# Coasting Along

D1567816

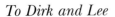

*To Dirk and Lee*

# Coasting Along

A Bicycling Guide to the New Jersey Shore, Pine Barrens and Delaware Bay Region

## Kurt B. Detwiler

**EPM Publications, Inc.**
**McLean, Virginia**

**Library of Congress Cataloging-in-Publication Data**

Detwiler, Kurt B.
    Coasting along : a bicycling guide to the New Jersey shore,
    Pine Barrens, and Delaware Bay region / Kurt B. Detwiler.
       p.    c.m.
    Includes bibliographical references and index.
    ISBN 1-889324-06-X
    1. Cycling—New Jersey—Guidebooks. 2. New Jersey—
    Guidebooks.    I. Title.
    GV1045.5.N5D48  1997
    917.49—dc21                         97-25540
                                                CIP

Book design and maps by Scott Edie, E Graphics
Cover photo by Janine A. Fisher

# *Contents*

# *Acknowledgments*

I wish to express my appreciation to the many people and organizations who helped with this project. Many New Jersey state, county and local agencies provided information and intelligent advice. At the state level these included the Department of Transportation, the Division of Travel and Tourism and Division of Parks and Forestry. Individual personnel at a number of state parks and forests, including Wharton, Bass River, Belleplaine and Lebanon State Forests and Fort Mott and Parvin State Parks, were generous with specific historical and ecological knowledge. Employees and volunteers at the Salem County and Cape May visitor centers helped with local expertise.

Thanks to my mother, Susan and brother, Dirk for their help and hospitality. Special thanks to Bill and Linda Leconey for their hospitality and to Janine A. Fisher for her photography. As always, thanks to my wife Jennifer for her patience and love.

Finally, thanks to all my New Jersey bicycling companions for showing me your favorite rides over the years in the Garden State.

# Introduction

This guidebook contains tours for bicyclists who wish to explore three distinct, yet related, areas of New Jersey. These three regions, the Jersey Shore, Pine Barrens and Delaware Bay Region, comprise a portion of the state's nine southeastern counties: Monmouth, Ocean, Burlington, Camden, Gloucester, Atlantic, Cape May, Cumberland and Salem. This is a low-lying, flat area bordered by the Delaware Bay in the south and southwest, the Atlantic Ocean in the east, and the New Jersey Turnpike on the northwest. Combined, the three regions contain over 3,000 square miles and represent about 40% of the state's total land.

I grew up and lived in this part of New Jersey for most of the first 29 years of my life. Riding along the Jersey Shore, through the Pine Barrens and Delaware Bay Region, I learned to love bicycling. This is where I went on my first long rides and completed my first century. When mountain bikes made it to the east coast I bought one and explored the region's unpaved roads and trails. This is where I learned about touring and took my first bike camping trips. Since 1979, I have bicycled thousands of miles throughout these three regions.

For novice and experienced bicyclists alike, the flat terrain, extensive road and trail system, natural beauty and interesting historical sites make all three regions ideal for bicycle touring. While the title, *Coasting Along*, refers first to the geographic location of the rides in the book because the three regions are located on the Atlantic Coastal Plain, it also refers to the act of coasting along on your bicycle and taking it easy. This is something I think you'll find yourself doing as you ride these tours.

Although there are other New Jersey bicycling books, some of which also have tours in these regions, I thought it was important to write a book that would concentrate on those aspects, both historical and natural, that make this entire area unique. I also thought it important to give more than a fleeting description of these historical sites and provide a sourcebook for bicyclists who want to learn where to look for flora and fauna. Previous bicycling books have, for the most part, ignored off-road tours. Given the popularity of mountain biking, I considered it essential also to include as many off-road tours as possible.

## *Jersey Shore*

The Jersey Shore extends from Sandy Hook to Cape May. It is best known as a resort area where millions of tourists come each summer to soak up the sun and relax. America's oldest beach resort (Cape May), as well as its most famous (Atlantic City), are located here. But the shore is also an area of rich maritime history, undeveloped island beaches and pristine wetlands.

At the shore it is possible to bicycle on a bustling boardwalk in the morning and ride through a remote wetlands refuge in the afternoon. It is not surprising that the bicycle is the most popular method of transportation at most shore towns. On a summer day you see every type, from clunky surfboard rack-equipped cruisers to sleek two-thousand-dollar racing bikes.

Many natural areas have been protected from development by the creation of federal, state and county preserves. A number of these are located along the wetlands and beaches of the Atlantic flyway, which is a critical migratory route for hundreds of species of North American birds. A number of museums and historic districts preserve the region's buildings, artifacts and

**The Cape May Lighthouse at dusk.**                    Janine A. Fisher

8

history from early whaling days, through the Victorian era to the heyday of the bayman. Throughout the region (including the Delaware Bay coast) is the New Jersey Coastal Heritage Trail Route. Established in 1988, it's a route system designed to acquaint visitors with New Jersey's natural and cultural sites. A joint project of the National Park Service and various New Jersey agencies, it is still under development. Though the trail is primarily designed for automobile traffic, many sites can be reached by bicycle. Look for the New Jersey Coastal Heritage Trail signs.

## Pine Barrens

The Pine Barrens is one of the world's most extraordinary ecosystems. It covers more than a million acres of upland pine-oak forests, lowland cedar swamps and slow-moving streams centered in Burlington County and including parts of Ocean, Atlantic, Cape May, Cumberland, Camden and Gloucester counties. Beneath the Pine Barrens is the 17-trillion-gallon combined Kirkwood Formation-Cohansey Aquifer. This is one of the largest sources of pristine freshwater on the east coast. Many animal and plant species are at the northern or southern limit of their range in the Pine Barrens. A number are among the state's and nation's endangered species, and a few species are found nowhere else.

Threatened with increased development in the 1960s, including a plan to build a jetport and a city with a projected population of 250,000, activists sought legislation to protect the area. Through the 1970s, a series of legislative proposals culminated in the 1978 creation of the federally-legislated, million-acre Pinelands National Reserve. A year later, New Jersey followed suit and created the Pinelands Protection Act, which includes a slightly smaller area. In 1983 Unesco recognized the area's importance and named it an international biosphere reserve. It is possible to bicycle for miles through the center of the preservation area without ever seeing another person. This is quite amazing when you consider that New Jersey is the most densely populated state.

Early settlers in the area started bog iron furnaces and forges, glassmaking factories and sawmills. In the 18th and 19th centuries, towns grew up around these enterprises only to be abandoned when factories and forges ceased production. Many techniques used in the commercial cultivation of blueberries and cranberries were pioneered here. The area is currently one of the leading producers of these crops.

Thousands of miles of paved and sand roads and trails abound in the area, making it perfect for both road and off-road bicycling. Routes take you by the location of many former towns, where today there is nothing except a clearing and a few ruins. You can explore the vast Pitch Pine forest, Atlantic White Cedar Swamps and sphagnum bogs. Depending on the season, you can watch cranberry harvesting or pick your own blueberries.

## *Delaware Bay Region*

The Delaware Bay Region comprises most of the southern-most area of New Jersey. This region contains extensive wetlands, unpolluted rivers and streams and secluded Delaware Bay beaches. Four rivers — the Maurice, Menantico, the Manumuskin and the Muskee Creek were recently designated part of the Federal Wild and Scenic Rivers Program. Thousands of acres of additional wetlands are protected by federal, state and local legislation. In 1992, much of this sensitive ecosystem was designated Wetlands of International Importance under the Ramsar Convention.[1] Every spring and fall millions of birds, including Ruddy Turnstones, Red Knots and Sanderlings, stop and feed here, making it one of the most important migratory bird sites in North America.

There is also plenty of history in the region. Some of New Jersey's oldest towns are located here, including Greenwich and Salem. More recent history is found at Mauricetown and Port Norris, formerly centers for shipbuilding and shellfishing. There is a preserved fort that once guarded the entrance to the Delaware River, a Civil War cemetery and some 19th-century lighthouses.

Bicycling in this sparsely populated and underappreciated part of New Jersey is a real pleasure. Routes run along secluded country roads past produce farms and orchards that remind the bicyclist why New Jersey is called the Garden State. You can ride on roads laid out in the late 1600s, lined with some of the best preserved 18th-century buildings in America.

And if you like birding, bring your binoculars, because you'll be riding to some of the best bird watching spots in the country.

These tours have been chosen according to a number of criteria including safety, scenic beauty, historical sites and yet other attractions. Rides vary in length and type of road and trail surface. All tours start from a public parking area (usually located at a park). Each section contains at least two rides from this common starting point. Usually the rides in each section can be easily combined to allow you to take longer tours. There are detailed directions, maps and historical and natural descriptions for each section. The appendix includes an event calendar, a listing of area bike shops and rental stores, as well as organizations, clubs and agencies. There is also a listing of relevant Internet resources and a selected bibliography.

# A Brief History

New Jersey and its residents have played a prominent role in the history of American bicycling. With the introduction of the high-wheeler around 1870 and the invention of the chain-driven safety bicycle a short time later, New Jerseyans, like many Americans, fell in love with bicycling. The state had dozens of clubs and activist groups that formed to improve and construct roads, organize races and develop safe routes.

In 1880, New Jersey cyclists won a landmark lawsuit against the Haddonfield Turnpike, which had banned high-wheelers in favor of horses and wagons.[9] A decade later, at the urging of cyclists, New Jersey became the first state to appropriate state money specifically for road improvement. Local groups, like the Cape May Bicycle Road Improvement Association, collected money to improve roads for bicycling. In just a few years the state's roads were filled with cyclists exploring country roads and riding to the shore.

When racing became popular, New Jersey and New Jerseyans went to the forefront of this new sport. From 1890-1910 the Millburn-Irvington race was one of the most popular road races in the country. The Newark Velodrome held many world level competitions. New Jersey produced two of the greatest early bicycling champions. Arthur "Jersey Skeeter" Zimmerman, born in Camden in 1869, was cycling's first international superstar. After winning hundreds of races and thousands of dollars in prize money, he retired to Asbury Park to run a hotel. Frank Kramer was born in Indiana but moved to East Orange, New Jersey, as a child. He won 16 consecutive national championships from 1901-1916. In 1912 he also won the world sprint championship.

Today, New Jersey still leads in bicycling. The U.S. Bicycling Hall of Fame is located in Somerville. Every Memorial Day weekend thousands of spectators line the town's streets to watch "The Tour of Somerville", one of America's premier cycling events. The state is a leader in the manufacture of dozens of high-tech materials necessary for the production of modern lightweight bicycles. New Jersey continues to produce a number of elite-level racers and has one of the strongest networks of clubs and advocacy groups in the country. As you ride these tours, remember the efforts of those cyclists who rode before you and take pride in New Jersey's place in bicycling's history.

# Bicycling Advice

Bicycling is a safe activity. Paying attention to equipment and following a few simple rules, can greatly reduce the chance of physical injury or discomfort. In addition to the following suggestions, it is essential to establish a rapport with a bicycle shop and its professional staff. Besides being the source of quality equipment and service, bicycle shops serve as important sources of information for the bicycling community. Shops often sponsor races, training rides and charity events. They can recommend clubs and rides that suit your style and fitness level too.

## Bicycles

Choosing a bicycle can be a complicated and highly personal decision and, sometimes, an expensive one. Rely on bike shop professionals to narrow your choice and find the proper size. Most off-road tours in this book will require a hybrid or mountain bike to traverse sand/dirt roads and trails. On longer road tours, you will be most efficient on a road bike but, of course, road rides can also be done on a hybrid or mountain bike. If you want to ride with someone, consider a tandem. Because the terrain is flat, many of these tours are great for tandems. For the same reason, recumbents are also a great choice for many of the paved road tours in this book. For the very short rides in this book you could even consider a single speed cruiser, but their heavy frames and balloon tires aren't much fun after ten miles or so. For children, BMX bikes are good for some of the shorter tours and a lot of fun off-road, although children should use a multi-geared bike for any longer rides. A good introduction to bicyling is the "half-bike" trailer, which enables a child to pedal behind an adult bike without steering.

## Equipment and Clothing

Bicycle safety begins with the bicycle helmet. There are dozens of comfortable, economical and effective helmets. Choose a helmet that matches your fashion style and have it professionally fitted. Wear it every time you get on your bicycle. A recent study by researchers at the University of Washington found that wearing a helmet lowers the chance of severe head injury by 74 percent. Other studies have claimed a prevention rate of over 85 percent.[3] These researchers also discovered that helmets significantly lowered the chance of upper and mid-face injury. New Jersey state law requires all children under 14 years of age to wear a properly fitted and fastened helmet.

Other bicycling clothing often appears strange to the novice, but it is very functional and adds to your safety and comfort. Shorts have padding that reduces chafing and numbness. If you feel uncomfortable wearing the form-fitting style, there are touring shorts that resemble regular hiking shorts. Padded gloves reduce hand fatigue and numbness. They also protect hands from abrasion in case of a fall. Bicycling jerseys have rear pockets and are made from lightweight, breathable materials. Shoes have reinforced soles and various pedal attachment systems to increase your comfort and efficiency. For colder weather there is a variety of clothing that provides comfort even when the temperature gets below freezing. I recommend carrying a bright-colored rainjacket with you on longer rides, in case of sudden storms.

Bicycle shops are covered from floor to ceiling with accessories. To help you choose from this baffling array, I have noted below those items that I consider essential.

To fix a flat tire and perform minor repairs you need to carry a repair kit, which should include a spare tube, patch kit, tire irons and a small assortment of tools. Inflating the tube requires a frame mount pump or compressed air cartridges. A water bottle and cage or a water pouch that straps to a rider's back are essential for providing comfort and preventing dehydration. A good quality lock is needed if you plan on leaving your bicycle unattended, even for a few seconds. Always use reflectors and put reflective tape on appropriate items, such as clothing, shoes and helmet. A good quality lighting system is required by New Jersey law if you bicycle at dusk or at night. A bell or other device capable of giving a signal audible for a distance of 100 feet is also required by New Jersey law. Bags (they come in various styles and sizes) are needed to carry the repair kit and other items. For carrying a lot of gear (especially if you plan on camping) a set of panniers is required. You should also carry these essential non-bicycle items: money, personal identification, pertinent medical information and a copy of this book.

You can also choose from a secondary list of accessories. Fenders eliminate most of the soaking associated with riding in the rain. Rearview mirrors provide more security for riding in traffic. Cycling computers not only provide mileage, but have various other features including average speed, current speed, maximum speed, elapsed time and on some models, altitude. A computer will allow you to keep track of mileage in the tour directions. An automobile bicycle carrier is a good investment if your trunk is small or you need to carry more than one bicycle. Optional non- bike items include binoculars, plant and animal field guides, a bathing suit and a camera.

To augment this guidebook's tours and maps, you might choose to carry other area maps. State and county maps are available from a number of agencies or through commercial publishers. Park and state forest maps can be found at most headquarters and some of the state forests sell United States Geological Survey quadrangle maps. Serious off-road riders should carry a compass and have orienteering skills.

## *Maintenance and Riding*

Beyond investment in the proper equipment and clothing, bicycle safety is dependent on equipment maintenance and proper riding behavior. Everyone should learn the  rudiments of bicycle mechanics and maintenance. There are a number of good books on the subject; shops and organizations conduct classes on bike maintenance. These basics, which include how to remove a wheel, repair a flat, install a chain and derailleur and brake adjustment, can be learned in a few hours. Before each ride get in the habit of inspecting the bike, paying particular attention to frayed cables, worn or under-inflated tires, dents or bulges in the frame or rims and out of true wheels. Lubricate and clean the bike at regular intervals. Once or twice a year, depending on your mileage, have your bike tuned up by a professional.

Proper riding behavior is essential not only to your safety, but to the continuing endeavor to give bicyclists the respect they are due. Bicyclists have a legal right to use most roads and trails, but with that right comes the responsibilty to behave properly. Poor behavior by a few bicyclists can result in increased motorist antagonism and the banning of bicyclists from off-road trails.

In general, road bicyclists in New Jersey are required to follow the same laws as all motorists. The New Jersey Bicycle Manual is available from the Department of Transportation, Motor Vehicle Services. Obey all traffic signs and lights. Ride with traffic and keep as far to the right as is safely possible. Ride single file and maintain a safe distance between you and the bicycle in front. Approach intersections cautiously and establish eye contact with motorists to determine their intentions. Learn and use the proper hand signals to indicate your intentions to others. In the area covered by this book, bicyclists are banned from the Garden State Parkway, the Atlantic City Expressway, Route 52 and the Route 18 Freeway and, of course, the New Jersey Turnpike and I-295.

Off-road riding has its own rules and etiquette. The International Mountain Bike Association has codified these rules:

- Yield to horses and pedestrians and signal your presence and intentions.

- Ride on open, established trails only and leave no trace of your presence.

- Keep your bicycle under control.

- Ride with a partner or tell someone of your itinerary and expected time of return.

## *Special Tips*

New Jersey has one of the best, most extensive road systems in the United States. Generally the roads in this guidebook are smooth, well-maintained and well- marked. Roads are also usually named in addition to having a route number; I have included both whenever applicable. The sand/dirt roads and trails that traverse the Pine Barrens, state forests and wildlife refuges usually do not have signs although they are often named on maps. Bicyclists have to rely on mileage, landmarks and other clues to follow directions in these areas. I have made every effort to make these directions as precise as possible, but because the terrain is flat and, to the unpracticed eye, can appear unchanging, it is necessary for bicyclists to pay attention when riding off-road.

Even though this is not the most populated part of New Jersey, traffic can still be heavy on some of these tours, especially in the shore towns between Memorial Day and Labor Day. When riding in these areas during this time, be especially cautious. Watch for turning and merging automobiles. Be aware that many people are on vacation and not familiar with their surroundings; unfortunately, some have been drinking alcohol. On many shore roads, and of course on boardwalks, you will be sharing the way with pedestrians and in-line skaters. Obey all local regulations regarding bike lanes, boardwalks and beach access.

Although the sand/dirt roads have very little traffic, be

aware that most are open to four-wheel drive automobiles; some trails are very popular with motorcycles and ATVs. If you hear them approaching on a narrow trail, pull over until they pass. Bicyclists are not permitted on the Batona Trail, the Pine Barrens main hiking trail, except where it coincides with historic sand/dirt roads. Access to other trails varies from jurisdiction to jurisdiction: inquire at the appropriate office before riding on these trails. Also be aware that thousands of acres of the Pine Barrens are privately owned. Do not trespass on private lands and roads.

If you are planning to ride on those roads and trails that have thick sections of sugar sand, choose the proper tire width and pressure. You will be most efficient on a mountain bike with wide tires set at a lower pressure for better traction. I like 2.2 inch tires set at about 40 p.s.i. Experiment to find the right combination for your riding style and weight.

Insects and ticks can be a problem in some of these areas. By taking a few precautions you can prevent tick bites (and Lyme Disease) and other insect bites. Use a repellent on skin or clothing. Be aware that repellents containing DEET have caused seizures in a few cases when applied directly to the skin. Wear light-colored clothing and tuck tights into your socks. Stay out of areas where there is heavy brush. After riding inspect your body and clothing for ticks. If ticks are removed a few hours after riding, there is no chance of the transmission of Lyme Disease. A brochure outlining Lyme Disease prevention is available at most park headquarters.

The Pine Barrens, in particular, is an area that is susceptible to forest fire. Talk to rangers and other personnel about current conditions. Although most of the state forests have controlled burning programs, fires can occur suddenly. Stay out of areas that are excessively dry and prevent forest fires by having camping fires only in designated areas and extinguishing them properly.

Bicycle safety and enjoyment are dependent on common sense and planning. Read each section and decide which rides match your skill and physical fitness level. Choose the style and type of bicycle, clothing and equipment accordingly. Once underway, use common sense, obey laws and ride courteously.

Although I have made every effort to make these tours as safe as possible, the final responsibility for safety is yours. The author and publisher can bear no responsibility for any accidents or injury incurred while following these tours.

# Map List

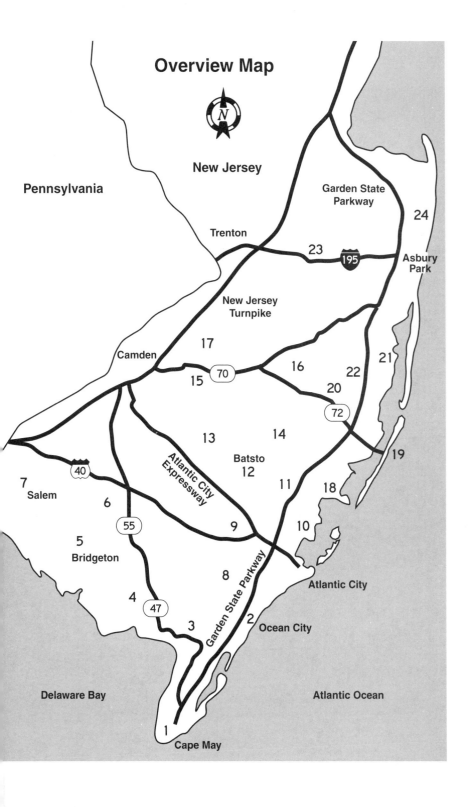

**A sailboat at sunset at Ocean City.**                    Janine A. Fisher

# Cape May, Cumberland and Salem Counties

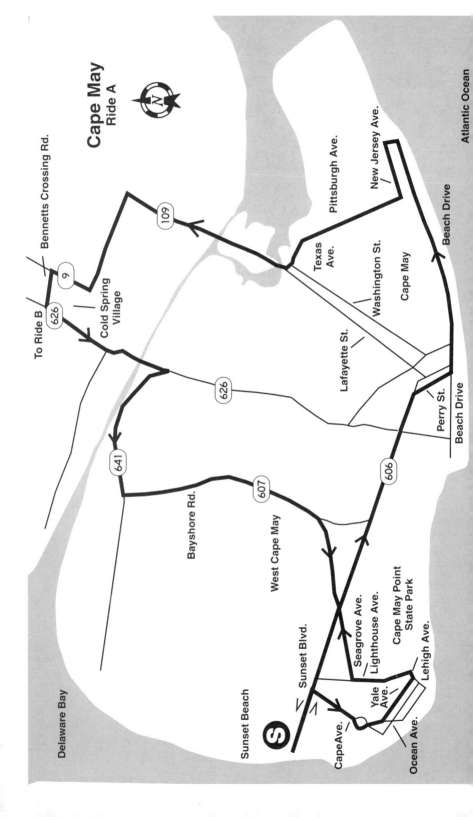

Cape May
Ride A

Bennetts Crossing Rd.

To Ride B

Cold Spring Village

Pittsburgh Ave.

New Jersey Ave.

Texas Ave.

Washington St.

Cape May

Beach Drive

Lafayette St.

Perry St.

Beach Drive

Bayshore Rd.

West Cape May

Sunset Blvd.

Sunset Beach

Cape Ave.

Seagrove Ave.

Lighthouse Ave.

Cape May Point State Park

Yale Ave.

Lehigh Ave.

Ocean Ave.

Delaware Bay

Atlantic Ocean

# The Cape

## Start:

Sunset Beach, Cape May Point, Cape May County. Garden State Parkway to its southern terminus. Route 9/109 west to Route 626 (Seashore Road). Left on Route 626, which is called Broadway in West Cape May, to Route 606 (Sunset Boulevard). Right on Route 606 to end at Sunset Beach parking area.

## Rides:

**Ride A** is 16.0 miles on paved roads with moderate to heavy traffic.

**Ride B** is 46.8 miles on paved roads with moderate to heavy traffic. The rides share common starting and ending sections.

Once you get to Cape May, take a hint from the locals and put the car keys away. The best way to see the town and get where you're going is by bike. In Cape May, there are more bikes than people, or so it seems. Bikes are crowded into racks alongside almost every guesthouse, bed and breakfast and oceanfront motel. This isn't a recent phenomenon; Cape May has attracted bicyclists for over 100 years. In 1896, Cape May had to set a town-wide speed limit of 8 m.p.h. because of the crowds of bicyclists. At that same time, some Cape May women started the Anti-Bicycle Club to protest the women who were participating in this "unladylike" activity.[4] I wonder what these spoil-sports would think about Lycra® shorts?

Cape May is often hailed as America's oldest seashore resort. Since the late 1700s, tourists have come here to be rejuvenated in this relaxing town by the Atlantic. Today visitors are attracted not only by the beach but by one of the finest collections of Victorian structures in the United States. There are hundreds of 19th-century buildings, ranging from gingerbread cottages to large hotels. Cape May is also the destination of bird watchers from all over the world. They come to view flocks of migrating birds that stop on the cape every spring and fall.

The rides go past a few of these birding spots, and continue through downtown Cape May. The routes then go north to Historic Cold Spring Village, where you can learn about 19th-century village life. At this point, Ride A returns to Sunset Beach while Ride B goes north through Cape May Court House before returning along the Delaware Bay. Use caution on these rides, because unfortunately not all have left their cars at home; there can be heavy traffic in some areas almost any time of year.

## *Directions: Ride A*

**0.0   Exit Sunset Beach east on Sunset Boulevard.**

The *Atlantus* broke free from its moorings and sank on June 8, 1926. Her concrete hull has been disappearing into the Delaware Bay ever since. The Sunset Beach Grille is a good place to get a snack before starting the ride. There are also gift shops selling the polished quartz "gems" known as Cape May Diamonds.

**0.3   Right on Route 651 (Cape Ave).**

Continue through residential area of Cape May Point.

There was a real dearth of imagination when it came to naming towns around here. Besides Cape May Point, you will ride by the location of old South Cape May, through West Cape May, Cape May, and Cape May Court House, which are all located in Cape May County, of course. All are named after Cornelius Mey, the Dutch explorer who sailed along the coast in the 1620s.

**0.8   Bear right at circle and turn right on Ocean Avenue (over half way around circle).**

**0.9   Four-way stop. Left on Yale Avenue.**

**1.3   Left on Lehigh Avenue. Entrance to Cape May Point State Park. Exit park to right on Lighthouse Avenue.**

The lighthouse beacon was first lit on October 31, 1859. The oil lamp was replaced by an electrical beacon in 1938. Its flash is visible 24 miles at sea. During World War II the lighthouse was darkened when submarine watchers manned the platform. If you have the time and inclination (and you're wearing the right shoes), pay the $3.50 admission fee and climb the 199-step cast-iron spiral staircase to the viewing platform. The view of the entire cape is great. Next, ride over to the visitor center. Again, if you have the

**The Dr. Henry Hunt House at 209 Congress Place is a typical example of the eclectic styles of the 1870s and 1880s.** Janine A. Fisher

right shoes and the time, pick up a trail guide, lock your bike next to the center and hike through the park's natural area. If you're here in the fall you might see people on the hawk watch platform looking for some of the 18 species that fly by this spot. Flocks of other species also congregate here, gaining strength before flying the 13 miles across the Delaware Bay on their way south.

**1.6   Right on Seagrove Avenue. Pavement is rough in sections.**

An excellent source for birding information and supplies is the Cape May Bird Observatory. To visit their office continue on Lighthouse Avenue and turn left on East Lake Drive.

Weatherby's Woods, which is part of the state park natural area, is to the right along this road.

**2.4   Right on Route 606 (Sunset Boulevard).**

On the right at 2.7 miles is the Cape May Migratory Bird Refuge. The Nature Conservancy owns this 187-acre site bordering the Atlantic. Once again, if you have the inclination, lock your bike near the parking area and hike the mile-long loop path. Call (609) 879-7262 for more information on this unique property.

The beach here is an important nesting spot for the endangered least tern *(Sterna albifrons)* and piping plover *(Charadrius melodus)*. Just offshore was the location of the thriving resort town of South Cape May. It was destroyed by a series of storms and the encroaching Atlantic.

**3.5   Traffic light. Continue straight at intersection with Route 626 (Broadway).**

Continue through West Cape May and enter Cape May.

**3.7   Traffic light. Right on Perry Street.**

There are a number of stores and restaurants in the Washington Street Mall. Most of the better-known Victorian houses and hotels are located in an area bordered by Lafayette Street, Congress Street, Franklin Street and Beach Avenue. Take a little side trip through this area, if you want, before continuing the ride.

Two good examples of Victorian architecture along here are the Pink House, c.1880 at 33 Perry Street and the Dr. Henry Hunt House, c.1881, just off Perry Street at 209 Congress Place. Many of these houses were built after 1878 when a fire destroyed 30 acres of the city.

**3.9   Traffic light. Left on Beach Drive. Continue straight through series of traffic lights.**

The promenade and the beach are on the right as you continue through town. If it's before 10 A.M. you can ride on the promenade and avoid the traffic. Make sure you have a beach badge if you want to take a swim.

**5.6   Bear left, now on Wilmington Avenue.**

**5.7   Stop. Left on New Jersey Avenue.**

**6.0   Stop. Right on Pittsburgh Avenue.**

The entrance to the Coast Guard reservation is to the right at 6.6 miles.

**6.8 Bear left, now on Texas Avenue.**

There is a convenience store on the right as you ride alongside the edge of Cape May Harbor.

**7.0 Right on Washington Street.**

**7.1 Bear left, then yield right onto Route 109 North (Lafayette Street).**

Most of Cape May's tour boats and fishing fleet dock here.

**7.1 Use caution crossing little bridge.**

**7.4 Use caution crossing larger bridge over Cape May Canal.**

**7.6 Continue straight on Route 109, at turn for Route 621. Watch for turning traffic.**

**8.0 Left on Route 109 north at entrance to Garden State Parkway (sign for Route 9). Use caution.**

**8.1 Stop. Continue straight onto Route 109.**

**8.8 Bear right on Route 9 north.**

The entrance to Historic Cold Spring Village is on the left at 9.4 miles. This recreated 19th-century village has a number of events from May through October. Events include a Civil War Weekend, a Festival of American Crafts and 19th-Century Harvest Days. The craftspeople and interpretive displays give a good view into the lives of 19th-century cape villagers. The ice cream shop and bakery is a nice place to refuel before continuing the ride. There is a small admission fee. Call (609) 898-2300 for more information.

**10.0 Left on Bennetts Crossing Road.**

Cross railroad tracks.

**10.0 Stop. Left on Route 626 (Seashore Road).**

Historic Cold Spring Village is now on the left as you return toward Cape May.

**11.2 Stop. Continue straight at intersection with Route 9, still on Route 626.**

**11.3 Bear left over Cape May Canal bridge.**

There is a wide bike lane on the bridge.

**11.8 Right on Route 641 (Higbees Beach Road).**

**12.9 Left on Route 607 (Bayshore Road).**

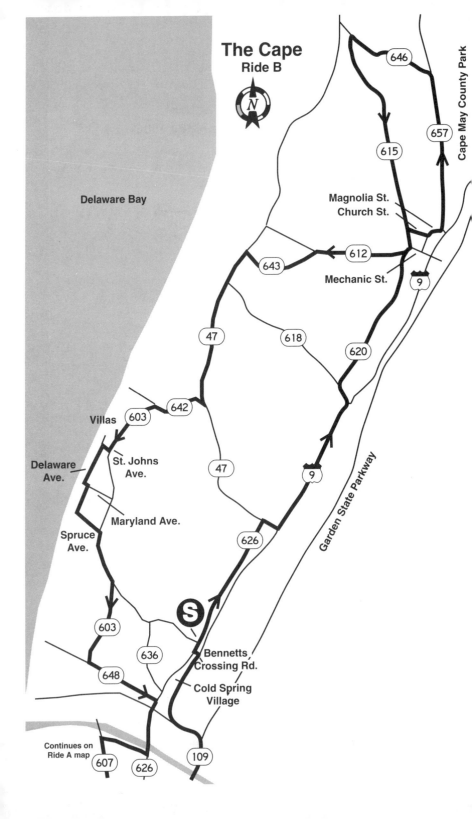

The farmland around West Cape May was once a center for growing lima beans. Every October the town hosts the Lima Bean Festival, where the Lima Bean Queen is crowned.

Most of the land to the right of this road is part of the Higbee Beach Wildlife Management Area.

**14.5 Stop. Right on Route 606 west (Sunset Boulevard).**

**16.0 Sunset Beach parking. End of tour.**

## Directions: Ride B

Follow directions for Ride A to 10.0 miles, then turn right instead of left on Route 626 (Seashore Road/Railroad Avenue).

**11.2 Traffic light. Continue straight at intersection with Route 613, still on Route 626.**

**12.7 Traffic light. Right on Route 47. Use caution—traffic.**

**12.8 Traffic light. Left on Route 9 north.**

**15.5 Traffic light. Left on Route 618 (Indian Trail).**

Cross railroad tracks at 15.6 miles.

**15.9 Right on Route 620 (Shunpike Road).**

This is a mostly wooded area.

**17.5 Four-way stop. Continue straight at intersection with Shell Bay Avenue, still on Route 620.**

**18.5 Stop. Right on Route 612 (Dias Creek Road).**

**18.6 Traffic light. Continue straight across Hand Avenue, still on Route 612.**

**18.6 Stop. Continue straight across Mechanic Street, now on Route 615.**

**18.7 Right on Church Street.**

Cross railroad tracks.

**18.9 Stop. Left on Magnolia Drive.**

**19.3 Bear left, still on Magnolia Drive.**

**19.3 Stop. Left on Route 657 (Dennis Road).**

**19.5 Traffic light. Continue straight on Route 657 at shopping center entrance.**

You can knock a few miles off this ride by turning at the bike lane that is on the left at 20.3 miles. It crosses to a sports complex on Route 615. Turn left on Route 615 and follow directions from there.

At 20.4 miles is the entrance to Cape May County Park and Zoo. There is a place to get snacks and to use public restrooms.

**22.0 Left on Route 646 (Goshen Swainton Road).**

**23.7 Left on Route 615 (Goshen Road).**

At one time, the Pine Barrens almost reached south to this point. To stem the tide of development, the federal government has acquired a number of acres and included them in the National Wildlife Refuge System. One such parcel is at 25.6 miles.

The previously mentioned sports complex is on the left at 26.0 miles.

**27.7 Stop. Bear right across Mechanic Street, now on Route 612 (Dias Creek Road).**

**27.7 Traffic light. Continue straight, still on Route 612, at intersection with Hand Avenue.**

**29.4 Left on Route 643 (Springers Mill Road).**

Another small National Wildlife Refuge is located across from this intersection.

**30.9 Stop. Left on Route 47 (Delsea Drive).**

Cross over Dias Creek. Yet another segment of the National Wildlife Refuge System is to the left.

You'll find a deli at 32.5 miles.

**33.7 Traffic light. right on Route 642 (Norbury's Landing Road). There is a sign for Villas and Fishing Creek.**

**34.7 Flashing yellow light. Bear left on Route 603 (Bay Shore Road).**

If you are riding in late May or early June you might want to continue to the end of Norbury's Landing Road to the beach. This is an excellent viewing area for the annual shorebird migration. There is an intepretive sign here describing the phenomenon. (See the Mauricetown section for more information).

Another deli is on the right at 35.0 miles. Continue across Fishing Creek, through a wetlands area into an area of houses and stores.

**35.9 Right on St. Johns Avenue.**

**36.0 Left on Delaware Avenue (Millman Lane). Road is rough in sections.**

Despite the lack of Art Deco hotels, this little town is called Miami Beach. There is a public beach access at 36.6 miles.

**36.8 Left on Maryland Avenue and immediate right on Beach/Delaware Avenue.**

Continue through town of Villas, along the Delaware Bay.

**37.3 Left on Spruce Avenue (a dead end is straight ahead).**

**37.8 Stop. Right on Route 603 (Bayshore Road).**

**38.2 Traffic light. Continue straight on Route 603, at intersection with Wildwood Avenue.**

**38.9 Right at intersection with Route 636, still on Route 603.**

**39.4 Traffic light. Continue straight at intersection with Route 613, still on Route 603.**

**40.3 Traffic light. Left on Route 648.**

Town Bank is one of the oldest towns on the Jersey Coast. Whalers came here in the 1680s from New England and built a dozen houses on a bluff overlooking the bay. Some settlers were descendants of Mayflower passengers. The original village site disappeared into the bay years ago.

**40.8 Traffic light. Continue straight on Route 648, at Taylor Road intersection.**

**41.4 Traffic light. Continue straight at Shunpike intersection, still on Route 648.**

**41.8 Right on Route 626 (Seashore Road).**

**42.0 Traffic light. Continue straight at intersection with Route 9, still on Route 626.**

At this point, follow the directions for Ride A from 11.2 miles to finish.

**46.8 Sunset Beach parking. End of tour.**

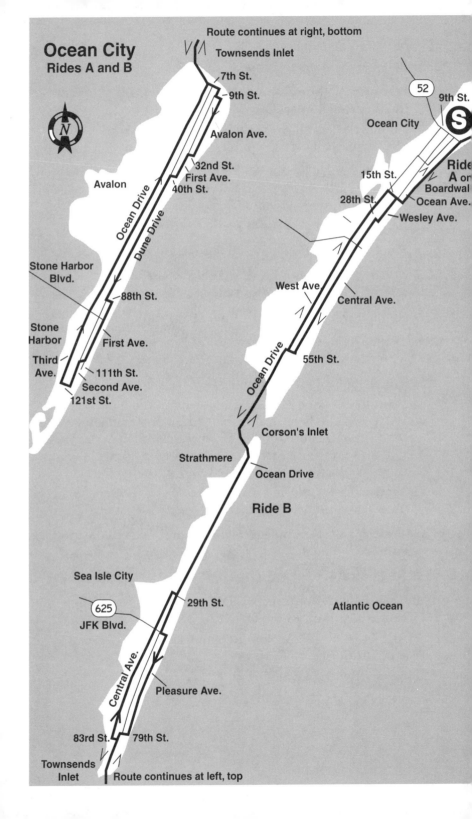

# Ocean City

## Start:

9th Street, Ocean City, Cape May County. Garden State Parkway to Exits 29 or 30. Follow signs for Ocean City. Proceed through traffic lights as Route 52 becomes 9th Street. Continue toward boardwalk. Parking is available on the street (Four-hour metered parking) or in a number of pay lots.

## Rides:

**Ride A** is 4.9 miles on a wooden boardwalk (pedestrian, bike and surrey traffic can be heavy in summer and on weekends).

**Ride B** is 42.6 miles on paved roads with moderate to heavy (summer) traffic.

America's first boardwalk was built in 1870 in Atlantic City. This elevated walkway enabled well- dressed Victorian ladies and gentlemen to stroll along the ocean without getting sand in their cuffs or long skirts and tracking this sand into hotel lobbies. It soon became one of the shore's most popular tourist attractions. Other towns followed Atlantic City's lead and today the boardwalk remains one of the Jersey Shore's most enduring symbols.

The Ocean City boardwalk is one of the nicest and most popular. There are a variety of landmarks along its 2.5 mile length, including the Strand Movie Theater, Shriver's Saltwater Taffy and the Music Pier. In addition, there are great views across the beach to the Atlantic Ocean just a hundred yards or so to the east. Whether you ride on your own bike or become a real tourist and rent a surrey to ride side-by-side with a friend, it is an enjoyable ride. Bicyclists are allowed on the boardwalk from 5 A.M. to 11 A.M.

The second ride goes through Ocean City, Strathmere, Sea Isle City, Avalon and Stone Harbor before looping back. It connects three separate barrier islands, crossing toll bridges over Corson's and Townsend's inlets (no toll for bicyclists). The main road along the southern shore is Ocean Drive (look for sign with seagull). It is variously called Central Avenue, Commonwealth Avenue, Landis Avenue and Third Avenue, but it is all the same. There are opportunities for bird watching at parks located at the inlets. If you have enough time, warm up by riding on the boardwalk in the morning, then ride the longer road route in the afternoon.

## Directions: Ride A

**0.0** **North (left) on boardwalk at intersection with 9th Street. Use lane designated for bicyclists and ride slowly and cautiously.**

Shriver's Saltwater Taffy, a landmark since 1898, is located here. The Music Pier is located a short distance to the right. Since 1928, there have been summer concerts in the pier's auditorium.

**0.4** **Left, then right onto narrower boardwalk section.**

**0.9** **Northern terminus of boardwalk. (Turn around).**

A lifeguard station is here. It has public restrooms. There is a bike rack if you want to lock up your bike and take a swim.

**1.3** **Left, then right as you return to wider boardwalk section.**

**1.9** **9th Street intersection.**

No surreys are allowed beyond the 2.2 mile point where the boardwalk narrows. The Ocean City Fishing Club Pier and 20th Street Pavilion are located along this stretch of boardwalk.

An historical marker describes the 1901 shipwreck of the Sindia just offshore at this point.

**3.4** **Southern terminus of the boardwalk. (Turn around.)**

There is a water fountain here.

**5.0** **9th Street intersection. End of tour.**

## Directions: Ride B

**0.0** **Exit parking west on 9th Street (away from boardwalk).**

**0.1** **Stop. Left on Ocean Avenue.**

**0.2** **Traffic light. Continue straight, still on Ocean Avenue.**

From its start as a Christian summer resort in the 1870s, Ocean City has been a family resort. Even today it is quieter than many of the other shore towns.

**0.7** **Bear to right, now on 15th Street.**

**0.8** **Flashing red light. Left on Wesley Avenue.**

**1.1** **Traffic light. Continue straight, still on Wesley Avenue.**

**2.2** Bear to right, now on 28th Street.

**2.2** Flashing yellow light. Left on Central Avenue.

**2.8** Traffic light. Continue straight, still on Central Avenue at intersection with 34th Street.

The beach is visible to the left as you continue south.

**5.1** Right on 55th Street (sign for Ocean Drive).

**5.1** Traffic light. Continue straight, now on Ocean Drive.

There is an ice cream parlor where the road bends left.

Ocean Drive leaves Ocean City and enters the Marmora Wildlife Management Area and Corson's Inlet State Park. This is a good bird watching spot.

**6.1** Cross bridge.

**7.1** Cross main bridge over Corson's Inlet. Use caution, narrow.

There is a toll plaza at 7.4 miles.

As you enter Strathmere, the Deauville Inn is located to the right along the bay. This is a relaxing place to stop for a bite to eat either now or on your return.

As you continue south along Ocean Drive, you pass a series of paths leading over the dunes to the beach. Strathmere has a very nice, usually uncrowded beach. At 9.2 miles you enter Sea Isle City.

**10.8** Traffic light. Continue straight, at intersection with 33rd Street, still on Ocean Drive.

Use caution through Sea Isle City.

**11.2** Traffic light. Left on Route 625 (J.F.K. Boulevard).

A number of restaurants and stores line this block.

**11.3** Stop. Right on Pleasure Avenue. Continue through traffic lights, staying on Pleasure Avenue.

**12.4** Stop. Left on 61st Street, then left again on Pleasure Avenue. Continue bearing left at series of side streets, still on Pleasure Avenue.

**13.3** Stop. Right on 79th Street.

**13.4** Stop. Left on Ocean Drive (Landis Avenue).

There are some delis, restaurants and markets along this road.

**13.7** Traffic light. Continue straight at intersection with 86th Street, still on Ocean Drive.

At 14.1 miles is Townsends Inlet Park. The park has a pavilion, restrooms and a water fountain. Interpretive markers describe the ecology of the coastal wetlands.

**14.2 Bridge over Townsends Inlet. Use caution.**

At 14.4 miles is a toll booth. Cross bridge to enter Avalon.

**14.8 Left on 7th Street.**

**14.9 Stop. Straight across Third Avenue.**

**15.0 Stop. Straight across Dune Drive.**

**15.2 Stop. Right on First Avenue.**

**15.3 Left on 9th Street.**

The parking area to the left overlooking Townsend Inlet and the Atlantic Ocean has become very popular with bird watchers. Every fall birders gather here to scan the ocean for seabirds flying south for the winter. Annually over a million loons, scoters and shearwaters and dozens of other species fly past this spot.

**15.4 Stop. Right on Avalon Avenue.**

There are pavilions and a small boardwalk to the left as you ride south.

**16.6 Stop. Right on 32nd Street.**

**16.7 Stop. Left on First Avenue.**

**17.1 Bear right on 40th Street.**

**17.2 Stop. Left on Dune Drive.**

Avalon has some of the highest dunes on the Jersey Shore. You enter Stone Harbor at 19.3 miles.

**19.8 Left on 88th Street.**

**19.9 Stop. Right on First Avenue.**

**21.1 Bear right on 111th Street.**

**21.2 Stop. Left on Second Avenue.**

**21.7 Right on 121st Street.**

**21.8 Right on Third Avenue (becomes Ocean Drive). Continue through series of stops and traffic lights as you return north through Stone Harbor and ultimately back to Ocean City.**

The Stone Harbor Bird Sanctuary is to the right as you continue past 117th Street. This 20-acre preserve is the country's only heronry located within a town's borders. Unfortunately for cyclists the best time to observe herons and egrets returning or leaving this roosting spot is at dawn and sunset.

There are a number of restaurants and stores along this road, also a bike shop at 23.0 miles.

**23.2 Traffic light. Continue straight at intersection with Stone Harbor Boulevard (96th St.), still on Ocean Drive. Continue through series of traffic lights through Avalon.**

About one mile to the left on Stone Harbor Boulevard is the Wetlands Institute. This non-profit organization has many educational programs about wetlands and coastal ecosystems. Call (609) 368-1211 for furthur information.

**27.6 Bear right, then left still on Ocean Drive.**

**28.3 Cross bridge over Townsends Inlet.**

At 28.6 is Townsends Inlet Park.

**29.0 Traffic light. Continue straight at intersection with 86th Street, still on Ocean Drive.**

**29.1 Left on 83rd Street.**

**29.1 Right on Central Avenue. Continue straight at traffic lights through Sea Isle City.**

**32.1 Right on 29th Street.**

**32.2 Stop. Left on Landis Avenue (Ocean Drive).**

**35.1 Bear left, still on Ocean Drive (sign for Ocean City).**

**35.3 Cross bridge over Corson's Inlet.**

**36.4 Cross second bridge.**

**37.4 Bear to right, still on Ocean Drive.**

**37.5 Traffic light. Left on West Avenue. Continue through series of traffic lights through Ocean City on this four-lane road.**

**41.7 Right on 15th Street.**

Continue through series of stop signs at cross streets.

**41.9 Bear left on Ocean Avenue.**

**42.4 Traffic light. Continue straight at 10th Street, still on Ocean Avenue.**

**42.6 Right on 9th Street. End of tour.**

# Belleplaine-Dennisville
## Rides A and B

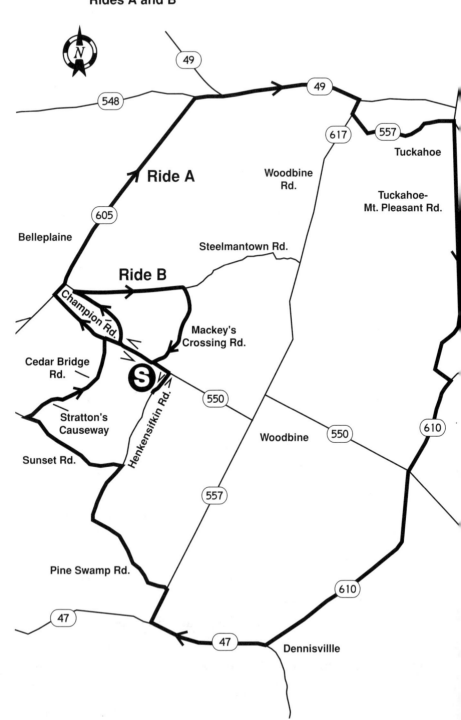

# *Belleplaine-Dennisville*

## *Start:*

Belleplaine State Forest Visitor Center, Belleplaine State Forest, Cape May County. From Garden State Parkway North take Exit 13, or from Garden State Parkway South take Exit 17. Proceed on Route 9 north to Route 550 west. Left on Route 550 through Woodbine to Route 557. Left on Route 557 to Route 550 west, again. Left at visitor center entrance.

## *Rides:*

**Ride A** is 28.2 miles on paved roads with light to moderate traffic.

**Ride B** is 4.5 miles on dirt and paved roads with light traffic.

Belleplaine State Forest contains almost 14,000 non-contiguous acres of pine, oak and cedar forest in northern Cape May County. Combined with nearby Dennis Creek and Beaver Swamp wildlife management areas, this is the southernmost pinelands area under state ownership. While soil conditions are marginally different from the core area of the Pine Barrens, this area contains basically the same flora and fauna and is considered part of the historical Pine Barrens.

Belleplaine was established in 1928 for timber management, water conservation and the development of recreation facilities. The area, which had been cleared of most of its timber, was reforested. An old cranberry bog was transformed into the park's centerpiece: 26-acre Lake Nummy. Civilian Conservation Corps workers also constructed dams, bridges and roads. Today the forest is one of the most popular camping destinations in South Jersey. If you visit in summer, bring a bathing suit to enjoy a swim in Lake Nummy after your ride.

Ride A leaves the park through the surrounding countryside. It goes past the small towns of Belleplaine, Tuckahoe and Dennisville. Ride B is a very short ride along some dirt forest roads. If you want to do some more extensive off-road exploring, forest maps are available at the park office. Inquire about current trail and road conditions, because some of them can be extremely wet and muddy.

## *Directions: Ride A*

**0.0  Exit parking to left on Henkensifkin Road.**

**0.1  Stop. Left on Route 550 (Woodbine Road).**

The Belleplaine Deli is at 1.9 miles on the right.

**2.1  Stop. Right on Route 605 (Tuckahoe Road). Eldora Road is to the left of this intersection.**

You ride through the small town of Belleplaine before entering heavy woods. Belleplaine means beautiful plain. Though fire is not as prevalent here as in most of the central Pine Barrens, a fire tower nevertheless watches over the area at 3.4 miles.

**5.4  Right on Route 548.**

**5.7  Stop. Continue straight, now on Route 49.**

There is a vegetable market on the left at 6.2 miles.

You are at the northern edge of Cape May County, and the Tuckahoe River is located a short distance north of this road.

**7.7  Right on Route 617 (Woodbine Road).**

The village of Marshallville is at this intersection. While there isn't much now, there were a few dozen houses and a large glass factory here in the 19th century. Ships were built alongside the Tuckahoe and launched from here, where they would sail into Great Egg Harbor.

**7.9  Left on Route 557 (Mill Road).**

Use caution crossing railroad tracks at 9.3 miles.

**9.6  Stop. Right on Route 664 (Tuckahoe-Mt. Pleasant Road).**

Tuckahoe was also a large shipbuilding center. In the 19th century, large sloops could navigate up the Tuckahoe River for ten miles from the Atlantic.

Use caution crossing railroad tracks at 10.1 miles.

**13.1  Stop. Right on Route 610 (Dennisville-Petersburg Road).**

There is a gravel quarry at 13.5 miles. Watch for truck traffic.

**14.7  Continue straight at intersection with Route 550, still on Route 610.**

This is the outskirts of Woodbine. Woodbine was started

as an agricultural colony in 1891 by Russian immigrants. Under the leadership of Hersch Sabsovich, the "colonists" cleared the area, laid out a town, constructed roads and planted hundreds of acres of crops. At the core of the community were twelve small factories and an academy, which focused on agricultural science. The town's street names, such as Shakespeare, Monroe and Adams Avenues, reflect the immigrants' commitment to education and their new country.

At 17.5 miles you cross railroad tracks and enter Dennisville, another of the many small towns in the area that relied on shipbuilding and the lumber industry. Ships as large as 1,000 tons were built alongside nearby Dennis Creek. Once completed, they were winched down the creek at high tide to the Delaware Bay. An interesting aspect of the lumber industry was the "mining" of cedar logs from the area's swamps. These huge trees had been buried in the muck for centuries. They were pulled to the surface, as unscarred as the day they fell. It is said that the shingles that once covered Independence Hall came from some of these trees.[5]

**18.1 Stop. Right on Route 47. Use caution—high speed traffic.**

Johnson Pond and Ludlams Pond are to the right as you continue back to Belleplaine. Dennis Creek Wildlife Management Area and the Delaware Bay are a short distance to the left.

**19.9 Right on Route 557 (Washington Road). There is a sign for the state forest.**

**20.3 Left on Pine Swamp road. (If you want to avoid this rough road, continue on Route 557 to Route 550. Turn left and proceed to the visitor center on the left).**

As you reenter the forest, you'll go through an area that was decimated by Gypsy Moths.

**22.7 Stop. Left on Sunset Road (unmarked).**

This road is smoother.

**24.7 Right (sharp) on Strattons Causeway (unmarked).**

The road narrows and gets rough in sections.

**25.7 Continue straight, now on Cedar Bridge Road (unmarked).**

**26.7 Stop. Right on Route 550 (Woodbine Road).**

**28.1 Right on Henkensifkin Road (park entrance).**

**28.2 Visitor center parking. End of tour.**

## *Ride B: Directions*

**0.0 Exit parking to left on Henkensifkin Road.**

**0.1 Stop. Left on Route 550 (Woodbine Road).**

**0.8 Right on Champion Road (unmarked/dirt). There is a gated, paved road on the left side of Route 550.**

This upland forest is mostly Pitch Pines. Timber stands in the forest are generally grown and harvested in 30-year cycles, although some of the forest dates from the 1930s and earlier.

**1.3 Bear left, still on Champion Road.**

**1.6 Right on Steelmantown Road (unmarked/dirt).**

If you continue a short distance on Champion Road, you will reach the small town of Belleplaine.

A section of this forest was harvested for timber after a Gypsy Moth infestation.

**2.7 Right on Mackey's Crossing Road (unmarked/dirt).**

**4.0 Stop. Left on Route 550 (Woodbine Road).**

**4.4 Right on Henkensifkin Road (sign for park entrance).**

**4.5 Visitor center parking. End of tour.**

**The East Point Lighthouse guards the entrance to the Maurice River.**

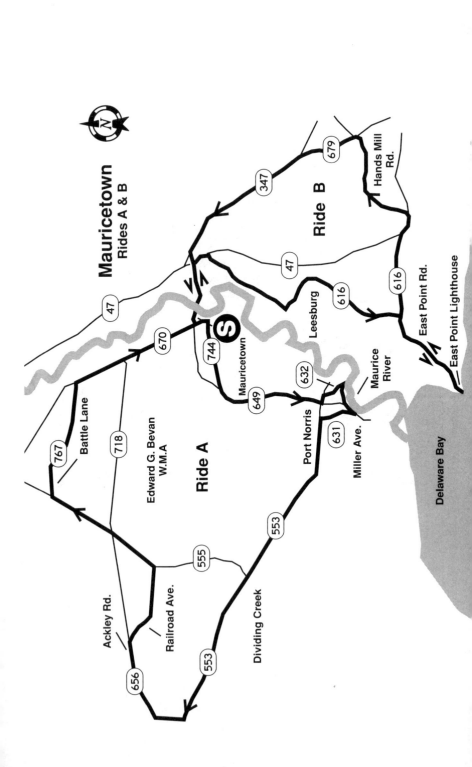

Mauricetown
Rides A & B

# Mauricetown

## Start:

Mauricetown River Park, Mauricetown, Cumberland County. Route 55 south to Route 47. Route 47 south to traffic light at Route 670. Turn right (west) and go over the Maurice River bridge. Turn left at flashing yellow light, south on Route 744. Turn left on Highland Avenue and go one block to Mauricetown River Park.

## Rides:

**Ride A** is 26.9 miles on paved roads with little to moderate traffic.

**Ride B** is 25.0 miles on paved roads (short section of dirt road at East Point Lighthouse) with little to moderate traffic.

**Ride C** is 34.7 miles on paved roads with little to moderate traffic.

The Maurice (pronounced "morris") River and its tributaries — the Manumuskin and Menantico rivers and Muskee Creek — form one of the most vital small watersheds in the Mid-Atlantic.

Fifteen threatened and endangered bird species, including the Bald Eagle, breed in the surrounding wetlands. Stands of wild rice attract migrating songbirds each fall. Pristine water flows south into the Delaware Bay, contributing to the health of crabs, oysters and other marine life. Near the mouth of the Maurice River millions of shorebirds arrive each spring to feed on Horseshoe Crab eggs. It is one of the most spectacular migratory displays in the Western Hemisphere.

From the 1880s through the 1930s, this area was considered the oyster capital of the world. Every fall hundreds of schooners would ply the Delaware Bay and Maurice River Cove, harvesting millions of bushels of oysters. In 1929 alone, 20 million pounds were harvested and transported by rail to Philadelphia and New York.

However the oyster population was decimated in 1957 by MSX (a protozoan parasite). Dermo (another parasite) has further affected the bay's oyster population, although some harvesting continues today. Despite these setbacks, the bay continues to be an important part of the area's economy.

Ride A goes along the west side of the Maurice River through Port Norris to the fishing centers at Bivalve and Shellpile. It continues west through Dividing Creek and returns through the Edward G. Bevan Wildlife Management Area. Ride B runs along the east side of the Maurice River through Leesburg and Dorchester, continuing to the East Point Lighthouse. Ride C goes through Port Elizabeth, along the Manumuskin River watershed and through the Peaslee Wildlife Management area. For a short distance, it goes through Atlantic and Cape May counties before returning to Mauricetown. More experienced riders can combine two or even all three of these routes for a full day of bicycling.

## *Directions: Ride A*

**0.0  Exit park toward Route 744.**

The Maurice River originates in Gloucester County, flowing 58 miles south into the bay. The remains of an original metal bridge are located at the park. It was hand-cranked open to allow passage of ships upstream.

**0.1  Stop. Left on Route 744 (Front Street).**

Mauricetown was originally called Mattox Landing. Before starting on the tour it is worthwhile to ride through the town's few streets viewing the well-kept Victorian homes and antique shops.

**0.2  Right on Route 744 (Noble Street).**

The white church steeple of the Mauricetown Church was a landmark for returning ship captains.

As you leave town there are ponds on both sides of the road. The road bends sharply to the right at 1.5 miles.

**1.5  Stop. Left on Route 649.**

**1.8  Stop. Left on Route 649 (sign for Port Norris and Bivalve). Use caution, moderate high speed traffic.**

**4.3  Stop. Left on Route 553 (Main Street).**

Port Norris was settled in the 1720s and was originally

called Dallas' Ferry. The construction of a rail line after the Civil War enabled watermen to sell their oysters in a timely fashion to Philadelphia and New York. In the late 1800s, there were almost 2,000 residents in town. It was said there were more millionaires per capita here than in any other town in New Jersey.

**4.4   Right on Route 632 (Ogden Street).**

There are seafood packing companies along this road.

**4.8   Right on Miller Avenue.**

This is the aptly named Shellpile.

**5.2   Continue straight, still on Miller Avenue at intersection with Memorial Avenue.**

**5.4   Bear right at Haskin Shellfish Research Laboratory, still on Miller Avenue.**

The Haskin Shellfish Research Laboratory is a Rutgers University field station. Scientists and students study shellfish and finfish, seeking cures for diseases and development of aquaculture along the bay. The research facility has over a 100 year history in New Jersey (one of the oldest facilities of its kind in the United States).

The marina has a number of working vessels moored here. Look for the *Cashier*. Built in 1847, it is one of the oldest working vessels in the country.

**5.5   Stop. Right on Route 631 (Shell Road/High Street). Use caution, watch for truck traffic.**

This is Bivalve. The Delaware Bay Schooner Project, dedicated to preserving the bay and the life of the watermen, is housed in the small building to the left. They have restored a schooner, the *A.J. Meerwald,* as a floating classroom. Call (609) 785-2060 for further information on educational excursions.

**6.2   Stop. Left on Route 553 (Main Street).**

At 9.8 miles the road goes over Dividing Creek. There is a boat rental shop, deli and cafe at this point. Thousands of acres of undeveloped wetlands stretch south toward the bay along this road. If you go south on Turkey Point Road you will be in a great bird watching spot. The road is rough in sections for the next few miles. At 12.6 miles you cross a small bridge. There is another boat rental shop at this point.

**13.9 Bear right, still on Route 553.**

**14.5 Right on 656 (Ackley Road).**

There is a country store at this intersection.

**15.0 Straight, still on Ackley Road (Route 718).**

The road is rough in sections. Use caution crossing railroad tracks at 15.3 miles.

**16.4 Right on Railroad Avenue.**

**17.1 Cross railroad tracks and bear immediately left. Use caution, truck traffic.**

The U.S. Silica Co. is located at this point. The large "dunes" to the right are the result of mining sand.

**18.3 Stop. Left on Route 555 — (Dividing Creek/Millville Road (unmarked). Use caution—cross railroad tracks.**

This road goes through the Edward G. Bevan Wildlife Management Area. You'll have mixed hardwood forest on both sides of the road.

**21.1 Right on Route 767, Battle Lane (unmarked).**

As you leave the wildlife area you enter development at Laurel Lake — including a pizza shop at 23.5 miles.

**23.9 Stop. Right on Route 670 (Buckshutem Road).**

There is a general store at this intersection.

The old village of Buckshutem was located along this road. In the 1830s it contained a few businesses and a dozen houses. A ferry ran from here to Bricksboro on the other side of the Maurice River.

**26.6 Stop. Flashing red light, continue straight now on Route 744.**

**26.8 Left on Highland Avenue.**

**26.9 Maurice River Park. End of tour.**

## Directions: Ride B

**0.0 Exit park to Route 744.**

**0.1 Right on Route 744 (Front Street).**

**0.3 Stop. Flashing red light. Right on Route 670.**

The bridge over the Maurice River is at 0.7 mile.

**1.8 Traffic Light. Right on Route 47 (Delsea Drive).**

There are two convenience stores at this intersection.

**2.1  Right on Route 616 (Main Street). Sign for Leesburg and Dorchester.**

Use caution at 3.0 miles crossing railroad tracks.

At 3.2 miles you enter Dorchester, a shipbuilding center since the 1800s. One of the oldest deepwater ship repair facilities in the Mid-Atlantic operates here. The river is visible to the right as you continue down Main Street.

You enter Leesburg at 4.0 miles. Leesburg also has a history as a shipbuilding town.

**4.5  Left, still on Route 616 (now called High Street). Follow sign for East Point Lighthouse.**

**5.7  Stay right, still on Route 616 (sign for East Point Lighthouse).**

There is a general store located in Heislerville.

**7.8  Stop. Right on East Point Road.**

As you enter the Heislerville Fish and Wildlife Management Area keep an eye out for birds, including the Bald Eagle *(Haliaeetus leucocephalus)* and Green-backed Heron *(Butorides striatus)*. In the fall this is a popular spot to look for migrating raptors.

Cross small bridge at 9.9 miles.

**10.3  Right on dirt drive to East Point Lighthouse.**

**10.5  East Point Lighthouse. Return to Heislerville on East Point Road.**

East Point Lighthouse is the only remaining lighthouse in Cumberland County. It was built in 1849 and is the second oldest lighthouse standing in New Jersey. For generations it guided watermen to the mouth of the Maurice River. Volunteers and donations are needed to help preserve this important structure. Write the Maurice River Historical Society at 210 N. High St., Millville, NJ 08332 for furthur information.

Every spring, thousands of Horseshoe Crabs *(Limulus polyphemus)* lay their eggs at waters edge on this beach. When the tide recedes the tiny eggs are revealed and migrating shorebirds descend for a feast.

These birds, including the Sanderling *(Calidris alba)*, Red Knot *(C. canutus)*, Ruddy Turnstone *(Arenaria interpres)* and Semipalmated Sandpiper *(C. pusilla)*, have migrated thousands of miles from Central and South America. Some have lost half their weight flying as much as 100 hours straight without a break. After a few weeks the shorebirds continue their migration to the Arctic tundra. Before they leave, they will have consumed 300 tons of the eggs.

The best time for viewing is usually from mid-May to early June. Do not go on the beaches to view the birds or you will disturb their feeding. The parking area, which is often filled with bird watchers observing the display, is the proper place for viewing. Call the New Jersey Division of Fish, Game and Wildlife at (609) 292-9400 for the location of other viewing areas and further information.

**13.2 Continue straight on Route 616.**

**14.9 Stop. Right on Route 47 (Delsea Drive).**

**15.5 Left on Hands Mill Road (sign for Belleplaine State Forest).**

**18.1 Left on Route 679 (Mosslander Road).**

There is a mixed hardwood forest on both sides of this road.

**19.5 Stop. Left on Route 347. Use caution, moderate high speed traffic.**

**23.1 Traffic light. Left on Route 670.**

**23.2 Traffic light. Straight at intersection with Route 47, still on Route 670.**

Cross Maurice River bridge at 24.2 miles.

**24.7 Flashing yellow light. Left on Route 744.**

**24.9 Left on Highland Avenue.**

**25.0 Mauricetown River Park. End of tour.**

## Directions: Ride C

**0.0 Exit park to Route 744 (Front Street).**

**0.1 Stop. Right on Route 744 (Front Street).**

**0.3 Stop. Flashing red light. Right on Route 670.**

**1.8 Traffic light. Straight at intersection with Route 47 (Delsea Drive), still on Route 670.**

There are two convenience stores at this intersection.

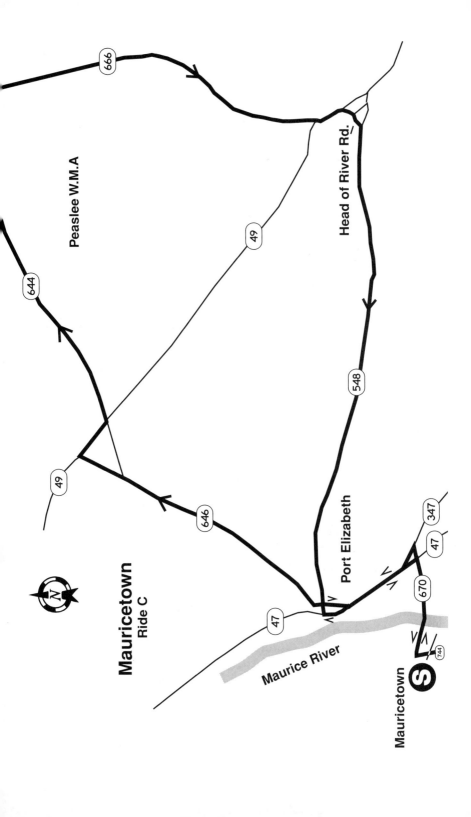

**1.9**   **Traffic light. Left on Route 347, immediately becomes Route 47 north. Use caution — high speed traffic.**

Cross bridge over Muskee Creek at 2.8 miles. Cross out-of-service railroad tracks at 2.9 miles.

Most of the rest of this ride is located within the Pinelands Protection Area.

**3.8**   **Right on Route 548 (Weatherby Road).**

This is the last road before crossing the bridge over the Manumuskin River.

Port Elizabeth is named for Elizabeth Bodly, who founded the town around 1780. Port Elizabeth was designated an official port of entry by Congress in 1789. The town flourished through the early 1800s.

**3.9**   **Left on Route 646 (Port Elizabeth-Cumberland Road).**

There are some old buildings along this road including the Eagle Glass Inn, which Christian Stanger opened as a small hotel in 1807. It is now a private residence.

**4.5**   **Bear left, still on Route 646. Straight ahead is an unnamed dirt road.**

This is a mostly wooded undeveloped area. Peaslee Wildlife Management Area is to the right along part of the road.

Although not visible from the road, the Manumuskin River is a short distance to the left. In 1986, a 3,000-acre section of this watershed was listed as a possible site for the storage of hazardous materials. Appreciating the pristine nature and ecological sensitivity of the area, local residents fought the project and got the Manumuskin, Menantico, Muskee and Maurice included in the federal Wild and Scenic River Program.

**8.4**   **Stop. Right on Route 49.**

**9.1**   **Left on Route 644 (Hesstown Road). In Atlantic County this road is called Thirteenth Avenue.**

A store marks this intersection.

The road continues past a few houses and reenters the wildlife management area. The forest is mostly oak with some Pitch Pines. After crossing the Tuckahoe River you enter Atlantic County.

**15.0**   **Stop. Right on Route 666 (Cape May Avenue).**

Continue through residential section in small town of Dorothy.

**17.0 Flashing yellow light. Continue straight at intersection with Route 637 (Cumberland Avenue), still on Route 666.**

Houses give way to woods on both sides of this road. At 21.5 miles you cross the small bridge over McNeals Branch.

**21.7 Stop. Continue straight at intersection with Route 649, still on Route 666.**

The Head of River Methodist Church, built in 1792, is located here. Head of River is so named because this used to be the navigable limit of the Tuckahoe River. It was a large shipbuilding center in the 19th century.

**21.8 Stop. Left on Route 49 (sign for Belleplaine State Forest).**

You cross over the Tuckahoe River at 22.2 miles and enter Cape May County.

**22.4 Right on Head of River Road (sign for Belleplaine State Forest). Immediately bear right away from state forest sign.**

**22.5 Stop. Continue straight, now on Route 548 (Weatherby Road).**

The Peaslee Wildlife Management Area is on the right side of this road.

Cross small bridge over Muskee Creek at 29.7 miles.

**30.8 Left on Route 646 (Port Elizabeth-Cumberland Road).**

**31.2 Stop. Left on Route 47. Use caution — high speed traffic.**

Cross over railroad tracks at 32.1 miles and then cross bridge over Muskee Creek.

There is a restaurant at 32.6 miles.

**32.7 Bear right, still on Route 47.**

**32.9 Traffic light. Right on Route 670.**

Cross railroad tracks at 33.1 miles. Cross the Maurice River bridge at 33.9 miles.

**34.4 Flashing yellow light. Left on Route 744 (Front Street).**

**34.6 Left on Highland Avenue.**

**34.7 Mauricetown River Park. End of tour.**

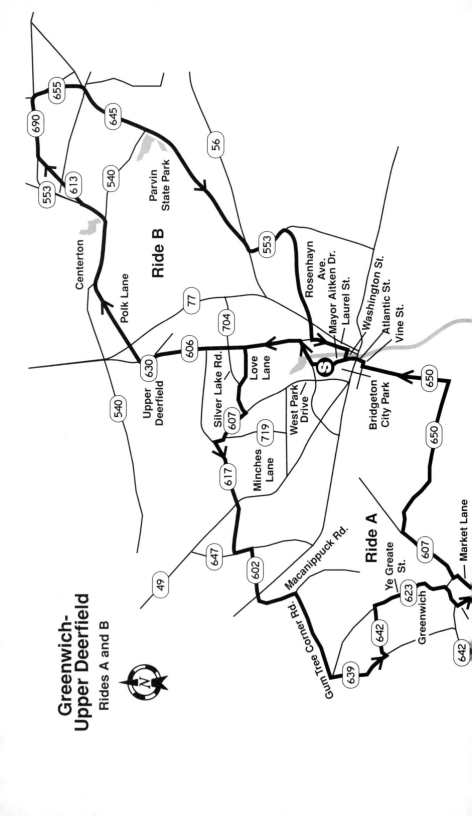

Greenwich-
Upper Deerfield
Rides A and B

Ride A

Ride B

Parvin
State Park

Centerton

Polk Lane

Upper
Deerfield

Silver Lake Rd.

Love
Lane

West Park
Drive

Minches
Lane

Macanippuck Rd.

Gum Tree Corner Rd.

Ye Greate
St.

Greenwich

Market Lane

Bridgeton
City Park

Rosenhayn
Ave.

Mayor Aitken Dr.

Laurel St.

Washington St.

Atlantic St.

Vine St.

655

690

645

56

553

613

540

553

540

77

704

606

630

607

719

617

647

602

49

639

642

623

607

650

650

642

719

# Greenwich-Upper Deerfield

## Start:

Bridgeton City Park, Bridgeton, Cumberland County. Route 49 or Route 77 to downtown Bridgeton. Follow signs to Bridgeton City Park. Parking is available adjacent to the Cohanzick Zoo on Mayor Aitken Drive.

## Rides:

**Ride A** is 29.9 miles on paved roads with light to moderate traffic.

**Ride B** is 27.0 miles on paved roads with light to moderate traffic. There are short distances of heavy traffic in downtown Bridgeton. Combining the two routes, including a short common starting section, results in a 56.9 mile ride.

A little more than a year after the Boston Tea Party, a similar event took place in Greenwich, New Jersey. On December 12, 1774 the captain of the brig *Greyhound* decided to put his cargo of tea ashore in Greenwich, when he learned that angry colonists threatened to destroy the tea if he docked in Philadelphia. It was secretly stored in the cellar of Dan Bowen's house on Market Square. However, local residents found out about the tea. On the night of December 22nd about 20 men, dressed as Indians, removed the tea and burned it in the square. Although some of the men were arrested and prosecuted, a jury of local citizens quickly acquitted them on the eve of the Revolutionary War.[6]

Greenwich was founded in 1675 by John Fenwick, who also founded nearby Salem. In 1701 it was designated an official Port of Entry of the Colony of West Jersey. Throughout the 18th century it was an important port, with ships carrying animal pelts, cedar shingles, corn and other items to the other colonies and the West Indies. Although the sloops are long gone, present-day Greenwich appears much as it did 200 years ago. One of the finest collections of 18th and 19th-century buildings in the Mid-Atlantic line Ye Greate Street.

In addition to Greenwich, these two rides give bicyclists the chance to explore a large area of northern and western Cumberland County and a small section of Salem County. This is an area of farms, historic towns and wetlands adjoining the Cohansey River, Stow Creek and Delaware Bay. Ride A goes north and west, before returning through historic Greenwich. Ride B goes north through the farmland of Upper Deerfield Township, continuing past Parvin State Park in Salem County.

Bridgeton has the largest historical district in New Jersey. The best way to explore the buildings in the downtown area is on a walking tour. Guides and furthur information are available at the Bridgeton/Cumberland County Tourism Center at 50 E. Broad Street. Call (609) 451-4802 for more information.

## Directions: Ride A

**0.0  Exit parking to right (north) on Mayor Aitken Drive.**

There is a restroom located near the parking lot. The waterway on the right, known as the Raceway, is popular with canoeists. You can rent a canoe at the nearby Bridgeton Pleasure Boat Company, located on Mayor Aitken Drive a short distance south of the zoo.

**0.3  Stop. Right on West Park Drive.**

Continue past Sunset Lake to the left.

**0.9  Traffic light. Left on Route 606 (Old Deerfield Pike).**

A deli appears on the right just after you turn.

**1.6  Traffic light. Continue straight at intersection with Cornwell Drive, still on Route 606.**

**2.5  Left on Love Lane (sign for Silver Lake).**

A small housing development circles the lake.

**3.2  Bear to right, still on Love Lane.**

**3.6  Stop. Cross narrow bridge at lake and bear left on Route 704 (Silver Lake Road).**

**4.3  Stop. Right on Route 607 (Beebe Run Road).**

**5.1  Bear sharply to right on Route 719 (Minches Lane).**

**5.4  Stop. Left on Route 617 (Columbia Highway).**

As you continue through the countryside, watch for several very old large trees that bear testimony to the age of the area's farms. As land was cleared, only a few trees were left near the farmhouses. Now many of the original farmhouses are gone, but the trees remain.

**6.8 Stop. Continue straight at intersection with Route 635 (Old Cohansey Road), still on Columbia Highway.**

**7.0 Stop. Continue straight at intersection with Route 49, still on Columbia Highway.**

A small food market is at this intersection, and to the south of it is the small town of Shiloh.

There is a community ballpark at 7.8 miles.

**8.3 Stop. Left on Route 647 (Marlboro Road).**

**8.8 Right on Route 602 (Buckhorn Road).**

**10.0 Continue straight at intersection with Route 626, now on Macanippuck Road.**

**10.3 Bear to left, still on Macanippuck Road.**

This is also an area of farms.

**10.8 Stop. Continue straight at intersection with Stow Creek Landing Road, still on Macanippuck Road.**

**11.1 Stop. Right on Gum Tree Corner Road.**

**13.4 Stop. Left on Route 639 (far left).**

This intersection is called Gum Tree Corner. At 14.6 miles cross the small bridge over Racoon Ditch. Osborne Fish and Wildlife Management Area is to the right. In May 1992, Delaware and New Jersey set aside 126,000 acres of valuable habitat along the Delaware Bay as a preservation area. Cumberland County has over 40 miles of Delaware Bay coastline, almost all of it undeveloped.

**16.1 Left on Route 642 (Bacon's Neck Road). (Sign for Hancocks Harbor to right).**

If you turn right here you can take a short side trip (about four miles roundtrip) to Bayside. Although little evidence remains, there were hundreds of small buildings, two large piers and a rail line at this point alongside the bay in the late 19th century. The chief industry was sturgeon fishing and the "harvesting" of roe. This activity gave the town its previous name of Caviar.[7]

**17.5  Stop. Right on Route 623. (Ye Greate Street in Greenwich).**

Continue as the road bends sharply twice entering town. Ye Greate Street was laid out by John Fenwick's executors, including William Penn, in 1684. It begins at the Cohansey River and runs for 2 1/2 miles, increasing in width from 80 to 90 to 100 feet. A ride along this historic street is a ride back in time. Historic markers explain the significance of some of the buildings.

**19.0  Right on Route 642 (Bacon's Neck Road).**

The Old Stone Tavern, built in 1748, is on the left at this intersection. The Wood Mansion, built in 1795, and the Wood Store, built in 1796, are on the right.

**19.5  Left on Pier Road.**

There are wetlands on the right as you approach the Cohansey River. A restaurant and marina, located alongside the river, make a relaxing spot for a ride break.

**19.9  Left on Market Lane.**

**20.6  Stop. Left on Ye Greate Street.**

The Tea Burning Monument stands on the left at this intersection, which once was Market Square. Besides being the location of the teaburning party, this is where area residents gathered for the Greenwich Fair every October from 1695-1765. Imagine an event that was already 70 years old, ten years before the Revolution!

If you want to continue to ride up Ye Greate Street before heading back to Bridgeton, the Gibbon House is located a short distance past the next turn on the right. It was built in 1730 and now houses the Cumberland Historical Society. Call (609) 455-4055 for further information.

**20.6  Stop. Right on Route 607 (Bridgeton Road).**

This road goes through a wetlands area and across a small bridge at 21.1 miles.

**22.4  Right on Route 650 (Sheppard's Mill Road).**

Farms and orchards line this country road.

**26.4  Stop. Left on Route 650 (Dutch Neck Road).**

If you turn left on Trench Road, you come to Dutch Neck Village, which has a restaurant and a number of small shops on the right.

**28.7  Flashing yellow light. Right on Vine Street.**

**28.8 Stop. Left on Atlantic Street.**

**28.9 Traffic light. Continue straight at intersection with Broad Street, still on Atlantic Street.**

**28.9 Traffic light. Continue straight at intersection with Commerce Street, now on Mayor Aitken Drive.**

In addition to the Cohanzick Zoo, the Bridgeton City Park contains two other interesting attractions. The Nail House Museum contains articles relating to the Industrial Revolution. Call (609) 455-4100 for hours and further information. The New Sweden Farmstead Museum is a recreation of a typical 17th-century village. Call (609) 455-9785 for hours and further information.

Use caution crossing the narrow bridge over the Raceway.

**29.9 Cohanzick Zoo parking. End of tour.**

## Directions: Ride B

**0.0   Exit parking to right (north) on Mayor Aitken Drive.**

**0.3   Stop. Right on West Park Drive.**

**0.9   Traffic light. Left on Route 606 (Old Deerfield Pike).**

**Ships have been docking at Greenwich for over 300 years.**

Deerfield Pike was an important toll road in the 19th century.

**1.6 Traffic light. Continue straight at intersection with Cornwell Drive, still on Route 606.**

The road gets hillier as you ride north from Bridgeton.

**4.7 Stop. Continue straight, now on Route 630.**

**5.2 Right on Polk Lane.**

Polk Lane has an impressive canopy of mature trees.

**5.7 Stop. Continue straight across intersection with Route 77, still on Polk Lane.**

Rutgers Experimental Research Farm, which contains 265 acres, is a leader in the development of better crops and agricultural products for South Jersey. It is located a short distance south of this road, along Burlington Road. Cumberland County has 99,000 acres of farmland and is often called the Garden Spot of the Garden State.

**7.5 Stop. Right on Route 540 (Deerfield Road). Use caution, there is moderate high speed traffic.**

Enter Salem County at 8.5 miles.

**9.1 Stop. Left on Route 553 (Centerton Road).**

Centerton Lake is on the left as you enter Centerton.

**9.4 Left, still on Route 553 (Buck Road).**

A store on the right and the Centerton Inn on the left occupy this intersection.

**10.1 Bear right on Route 613 (Centerton-Porchtown Road).**

**10.6 Continue straight at intersection with Brotmanville Road, still on Route 613.**

The road is a little rough in sections.

**11.7 Right on Route 690 (Willow Grove Road).**

**13.0 Right on Route 655 (Alvine Road).**

**14.4 Stop. Right on Route 645 (Parvin's Mill Road).**

This intersection is called Six Points. The road goes through a small pine forest on the way to the park.

**16.4 Stop. Continue straight at intersection with Route 540, still on Route 645.**

If you turn right, Parvin State Park Visitor Center is 0.2 mile on the left. (See the Parvin State Forest section for more information).

As you continue on Route 645, you pass Parvin Lake, then the smaller Thundergust Lake.

**17.6 Four-way stop. Continue straight at intersection with Route 634 (unmarked), still on Route 645.**

**18.2 Stop. Continue straight at intersection with Route 658 (unmarked), still on Route 645.**

There are a number of farms along this road.

**20.6 Stop. Right on Route 56.**

**20.7 Traffic light. Left on Route 553 (South Woodruff Road).**

The Woodruff United Methodist Church c.1870, is on the right at this intersection. Cross railroad tracks at 21.1 miles.

**21.9 Bear right and stop. Right on Route 659 (Rosenhayn Avenue).**

As this road reenters Bridgeton, watch for more traffic. Cross two railroad tracks at 24.3 miles.

**24.5 Traffic light. Continue straight at intersection with Route 77, still on Rosenhayn Avenue.**

**24.9 Left on Laurel Street. Continue through two traffic lights, still on Laurel street.**

**25.9 Traffic light. Right on Washington Street.**

Cross the Cohansey River and enter Bridgeton City Park.

**26.1 Stop. Right on Mayor Aitken Drive.**

**27.0 Cohanzick Zoo parking. End of tour.**

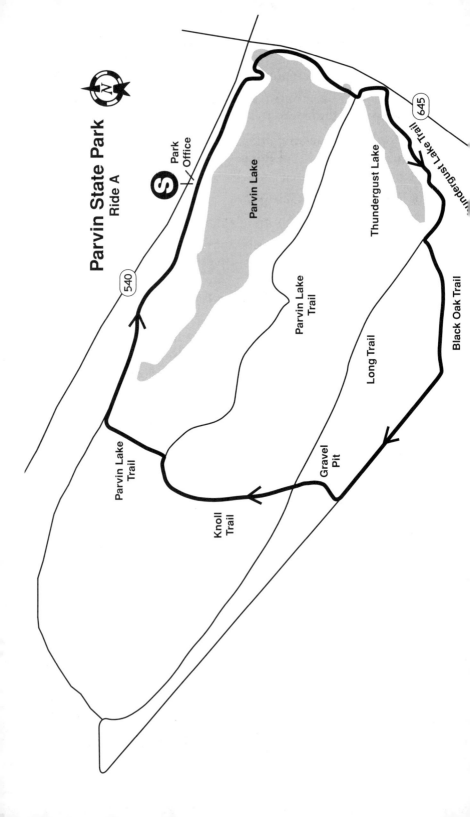

# Parvin State Park
## Ride A

N

540

Park Office
S

Parvin Lake

Parvin Lake Trail

Knoll Trail

Gravel Pit

Long Trail

Thundergust Lake

Black Oak Trail

Thundergust Lake Trail

645

Parvin Lake Trail

# Parvin State Park

## Start:

Parvin State Park office, Parvin State Park, Salem County. Route 55 to Exit 35. Route 674 west to Six Points. Left on Route 645 to Route 540. Right on Route 540 to parking across from park office and Parvin Lake beach. (If this lot is full there are other parking areas along Route 645).

## Rides:

**Ride A** is 4.3 miles on dirt/sand park trails.

**Ride B** is 18.8 miles on paved roads with light to moderate traffic.

Until the mid-19th century the Pine Barrens extended into this area of eastern Salem and northern Cumberland counties. There were thousands of acres of pine/oak fringe forest and cedar swamp lowlands extending almost to Bridgeton. However, with the growth of Millville and Vineland and surrounding agricultural development, much of the habitat was altered. Parvin State Forest contains one of the few large sections (1,135 acres) of remaining pinelands habitat in the area. Other pockets exist around Union, Centerton, Rainbow and Willow Grove lakes which, along with Parvin Lake, were all formed by damming the Maurice River and its tributaries.

With this development of agriculture, a number of different ethnic groups have lived in this area. In the 1880s, the Hebrew Immigrant Society founded a planned agricultural community at Alliance for recent Russian and Polish immigrants. After its success, other communities started at Brotmanville, Norma, Rosenhayn and Carmel. In addition to farming, the communities had small garment and craft factories.

During World War II, nearby Seabrook Farms needed farmhands and processing workers. Under the War Relocation Authority, 500 Japanese families were forcibly moved to the area. Some of the park's facilities were used for a summer camp for the children. German prisoners of war were also briefly confined here and worked in nearby farms. After the war, refugees from Eastern Europe and Kalmycks from Mongolia lived in transition housing, while awaiting final settlement. The best source of information on this fascinating history is the Upper Deerfield Museum, located north of Bridgeton on Route 77. Call (609) 451-8393 for more information.

Ride A is a short ride along some of the park's trails. Get a map from the park office if you want to do some more exploring. Of the approxiamately 15 miles of trails, I've found about ten miles good for biking. Ride B leaves the park going north to Willow Grove Lake. It returns through the surrounding farmland and the aforementioned towns of Brotmanville, Norma, Carmel and Rosenhayn. Boating, fishing, camping and swimming are also very popular at this well-maintained state park.

## Directions: Ride A

**0.0**  **Exit park office area to left (as you face Parvin Lake) on Parvin Lake Trail (green blazes).**

Cross small bridge at 0.2 mile and second bridge at 0.3 mile. Walk bike down stairs on second bridge.

Continue around spillway alongside Route 645 (Parvin's Mill Road).

**0.4**  **Bear right on Parvin Lake Trail through Fishermen's Landing parking area.**

Parvin Lake was originally created in the late 18th century by Lemuel Parvin, who dammed Muddy Run to power a sawmill. The state started acquiring the land in the 1930s.

**0.5**  **Cross small footbridge, keep straight across paved park road and bear left at edge of Thundergust Lake on Thundergust Lake Trail.**

**0.7**  **Bear right, still on Thundergust Lake Trail.**

Continue with Thundergust Lake on your right and parking/picnic area on the left. Thundergust Lake was created in the 1930s by the Civilian Conservation Corps.

**1.2**  **Use caution crossing small footbridge over Thundergust Brook.**

**1.2**  **Left on Black Oak Trail (unmarked). Straight at this point is Long Trail.**

This trail can have some very wet sections. The woods, very similar to those at the core of the Pine Barrens, are full of Pitch Pines (*Pinus rigida*), Mountain-laurel (*Kalmia latifolia*) and American Holly (*Ilex opaca*).

**2.2    Right on unmarked/unnamed trail. This is the first crossing over Black Oak Trail.**

Ride down small hill through a gravel pit.

**2.3    Left on Knoll Trail (unmarked). If you reach a paved forest road you've gone too far.**

This narrow trail continues through an uplands area.

**2.6    Cross Forest Loop Road (paved).**

Knoll Trail continues through a swampy area. You cross small walkways at 2.8 and 2.9 miles.

**3.0    Cross Forest Loop Road (paved).**

**3.1    Left on Parvin Lake Trail (rough pavement). A green arrow is painted on the pavement.**

(If you want, you can continue straight, following green blazes through Jaggers Point Camping, alongside lake to Fishermen's Landing. Retrace route back to park office.) You continue across Muddy Run through a lowlands area.

The park's largest stands of Atlantic White Cedar (*Chamaecyparis thyoides*) line Muddy Run and the little streams that feed it.

**3.3    Right on Parvin Lake Trail (green blazes).**

If you're riding in summer, you'll hear the sounds of laughing and splashing as you approach Parvin Lake bathing beach.

**4.3    Park office on right. End of tour.**

## *Ride B: Directions*

**0.0    Exit park office to right (east) on Route 540.**

**0.2    Left on Route 645 (Parvin's Mill Road).**

The pine/oak forest around the park gives way to an area of farmland.

**2.0    Stop. Continue straight on Route 645, at Six Points intersection (sign for Willow Grove).**

**4.1    Right on Route 638 (Jesse Bridge Road).**

For a view of picturesque Willow Grove Lake continue on

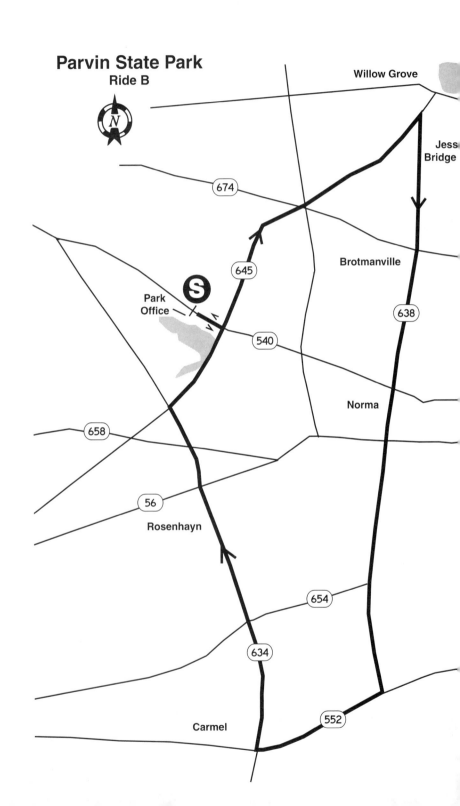

# Parvin State Park
### Ride B

Route 645 for 0.1 mile. Turn right on Route 639. The lake appears shortly on the left. When you see it, you understand why the Nature Conservancy has purchased property around it for a preserve. The Maurice River flows south from here.

**6.0 Stop. Continue straight at intersection with Route 674 (Garden Rd.), still on Route 638 (now called Gershel Ave.).**

This is Brotmanville, one of the 19th-century Jewish agricultural communites. There is an historic cemetery on the left at 7.2 miles.

**7.6 Stop. Continue straight at Route 540 intersection, still on Gershel Avenue.**

This small crossroads is Norma.

**8.3 Traffic light. Continue straight at intersection with Route 56, still on Route 638.**

Immediately cross railroad tracks. There are large farms and a mixed pine/oak forest along this road.

**11.4 Stop. Right on Route 552.**

Union Lake Fish and Wildlife Area is located across from the intersection. Union Lake was also created by damming the Maurice River.

**13.1 Flashing yellow light. Right on Route 634 (Morton Avenue).**

Carmel has the only Orthodox synagogue still in regular use in the area. Built between 1901-1907, the Beth Hillel Synagogue is located just beyond this intersection.

There are farms and houses along this road. The Deerfield Twp. School is on the left at 15.0 miles.

**15.8 Flashing yellow light. Continue straight at Route 659, still on Route 634.**

A general store is located at 16.0 miles on the left, 0.2 mile before the railroad tracks.

**16.4 Traffic light. Continue straight at intersection with Route 56, still on Route 634.**

**16.9 Stop. Continue straight across Route 658, still on Route 634 (Morton Avenue).**

**17.5 Four-way stop. Right on Route 645 (Parvin's Mill Road).**

Parvin State Park is on left as you reenter Salem County.

**18.6 Stop. Left on Route 540.**

**18.8 Park office on left. End of tour.**

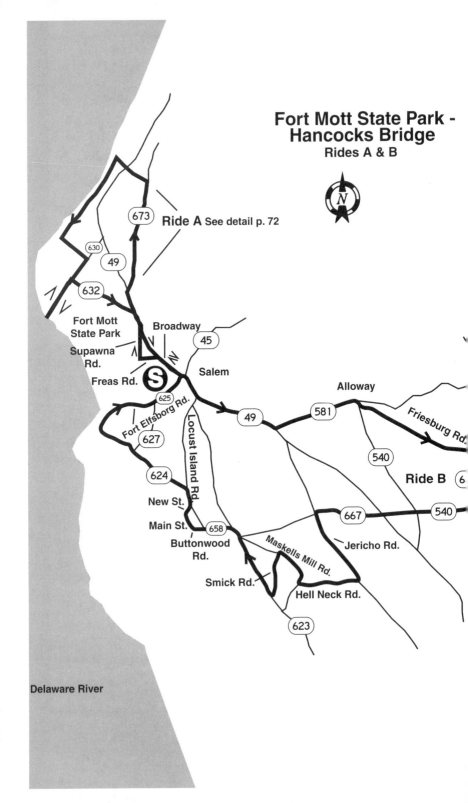

# Fort Mott State Park - Hancocks Bridge
## Rides A & B

**Ride A** See detail p. 72

673

630

49

632

**Fort Mott State Park**

Broadway

45

Supawna Rd.

Salem

Freas Rd.

**S**

625

Fort Eltsborg Rd.

627

Locust Island Rd.

49

581

Alloway

Friesburg Rd.

540

**Ride B** 6

624

540

New St.

Main St.

658

667

Jericho Rd.

Buttonwood Rd.

Maskells Mill Rd.

Smick Rd.

Hell Neck Rd.

623

Delaware River

# *Fort Mott State Park - Hancocks Bridge*

## *Start:*

Salem, Salem County. South on Route 49 or Route 45 to downtown Salem. Free public parking is available throughout town. Tours start at the Old Oak Tree located in the Friends Burial Ground on Route 49 (West Broadway).

## *Rides:*

**Ride A** is 21.4 miles on paved roads with moderate traffic.

**Ride B** is 38.5 miles on paved roads with light to moderate traffic. Rides can be easily combined, resulting in a 59.9 mile ride.

There is nothing quite like a vine-ripened Jersey tomato. I don't know whether it is South Jersey's flat, sandy soil or its latitude, but the tomatoes grown here are (forgive this native son's hyperbole) the tastiest in the world.

According to local lore, Salem resident Robert Gibbon Johnson was directly responsible for the start of the area's tomato industry. Even though in the 1800s, the tomato had been cultivated and eaten for centuries in South America and Europe, the plant was not yet popular in the United States. The few available varieties produced highly acidic and pulpy fruit and some people even thought the plant was poisonous. In 1820, Johnson, who was president of the New Jersey Agricultural Society, made a public display of eating a tomato he had grown from a South American seed to prove that it wasn't poisonous, and to encourage local farmers to grow the plant. With the introduction of tastier varieties and the simultaneous development of marl as a fertilizer, the tomato soon became the most popular crop of the area. By 1900, more than 30 canneries and catsup factories dotted the county.

In season, you can buy tomatoes and other produce from farmers who set up small stands or park their pick-up trucks alongside many of the country roads on these routes. In addition, the rides go by some of the more interesting historical sites in the county.

Ride A goes through Pennsville along the Delaware River to Fort Mott State Park and Finn's Point National Cemetery. Ride B goes through the rolling countryside east of town to Quinton and Hancocks Bridge, two Revolutionary War sites.

Start your visit at the Salem County Chamber of Commerce at the corner of Market Street and Broadway. The office has more information on historical sites and county maps. Call (609) 935-1415.

## Directions: Ride A

**0.0  Start tour on Broadway (Route 49) at the Friends Burial Ground. Go west on Broadway.**

The Old Oak Tree in the burial ground is estimated to be over 500 years old and its branches cover one-quarter acre. Here, in 1675, John Fenwick purchased what is today Cumberland and Salem counties from the Lenni-Lenape Indians. Fenwick's communities at Salem and Greenwich were the first permanent English-speaking settlements on the Delaware River. Members of the original settlement are buried here in unmarked graves.

**0.3  Traffic light. Right on Route 49 west (Front Street).**

There is a deli/food market at this intersection.

Use caution crossing two railroad tracks at 0.4 mile.

**0.5  Bear left, still on Route 49 west.**

Use caution crossing the bridge over the Salem River. As you leave Salem you'll see a marina on the left.

**3.5  Traffic light. Right on Route 673 (Hook Road). Sign for the Delaware Memorial Bridge.**

As you ride north, through wetlands and open fields, you'll see a hunting club at 4.5 miles.

**6.9  Left on Churchtown Road.**

Continue through this residential section of Pennsville.

**7.9  Stop. Right on Route 49 (Broadway).**

**7.9  Left on Church Landing Road. Use caution turning on Route 49.**

St. Georges Church and cemetery are at this intersection. The church, which contains artifacts from an early

Swedish settlement, dates from 1808. It replaced an earlier structure that was built in 1717.

**8.3 Left on North River Drive.**

Before turning, continue a short distance to the end of Church Landing Road. On the right is the Farmstead Museum c.1860, which serves as the headquarters of the Penns Grove Historical Society.

There is an excellent view of the Delaware Memorial Bridge from the beach at the end of the road. The bridge, at 2150 feet, is one of the longest twin span bridges in the world. This small beach is a good place for a ride break. An historical marker explains how early settlers had to make a perilous boat trip every week to attend church in Wilmington.

There are views of the Delaware River to the right as you continue south through this nice neighborhood.

**9.5 Continue straight through gate after intersection with Lakeview Ave.**

**9.5 Bear right on short path to path along seawall in Riverview Park.**

Continue along seawall promenade south through park. Public restrooms are located in Riverview Park.

**9.9 Continue through Riverview Inn parking lot at the end of the park.**

**9.9 Stop. Continue straight onto Enlow Place Road.**

**10.2 Left on Highland Ave.**

**10.2 Right on Riviera Drive.**

A deli and store are located at this intersection. Open fields to the right offer good river views.

**11.2 Road bends to left, becomes Industrial Park Road.**

**12.8 Stop. Right on Route 630 (Fort Mott Road).**

**13.5 Continue straight at intersection with Route 632, still on Route 630.**

**13.8 Stop. Continue to right still on Route 630. (Coastal Heritage sign).**

To the right is the Killcohook National Wildlife Refuge.

**14.7 Enter Fort Mott State Park. Continue to parking area and**

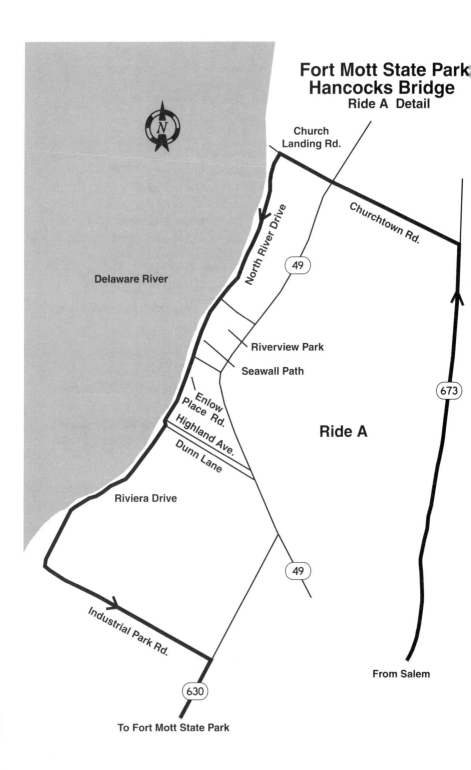

**Fort Mott State Park/
Hancocks Bridge**
Ride A  Detail

Church
Landing Rd.

Churchtown Rd.

North River Drive

49

Delaware River

Riverview Park

Seawall Path

Enlow
Place  Rd.

Highland Ave.

Dunn Lane

**Ride A**

673

Riviera Drive

49

Industrial Park Rd.

From Salem

630

To Fort Mott State Park

**fort entrance at 21.8 miles. Exit park back on Route 630.**

Fort Mott was planned as part of America's coastal defense after the Civil War. Construction was completed in 1896 in anticipation of the Spanish-American War. The Fort is named for General Gershom Mott, commander of the New Jersey Volunteers in the Civil War. Adjacent to the parking area is a picnic pavilion and public restrooms.

As you leave the fort, Finn's Point National Cemetery, dedicated in 1875, is located to the left. Finn's Point contains the remains of 2,400 Confederate soldiers who died while imprisoned at Fort Delaware, which was located on Pea Patch Island. Confederates died in large numbers from disease and malnutrition, including scurvy. Their bodies were rowed ashore here and buried; 300 Union soldiers are also buried here.

**16.1 Bear right on Route 632 (Lighthouse Road). Continue past lighthouse to right.**

Finn's Point Range Light, a unique wrought iron structure built in 1876, stands at the intersection. The marker tells you that a rear range light was aligned with another light to allow navigators to determine the exact position of their ship in the Delaware Bay.

This road continues through the wetlands of the Supawna Wildlife Refuge.

**18.4 Stop. Right on Route 49. Use caution, there is moderate high speed traffic.**

**18.5 Right on Supawna Road. Road is a little rough and narrow.**

**19.3 Left on Freas Road.**

**19.7 Stop. Right on Route 49.**

Use caution over Salem River Bidge (steel grating) at 20.8 miles.

**20.9 Bear right, still on Route 49 (Front Street).**

**21.1 Traffic light. Left on West Broadway (sign for Route 49 east).**

**21.4 Old Oak Tree and Friends Burial Ground on left. End of tour.**

# Directions: Ride B

**0.0**  **East on Broadway.**

**0.2**  **Traffic light. Continue straight at intersection with Market Street, still on Broadway.**

Market Street contains a number of Salem's most important historical buildings. The Old Court House, built in 1735, is at the intersection.

**0.3**  **Traffic light. Continue straight at intersection with Seventh Street, still on Broadway.**

Just before Seventh Street, on the left, is the Friends Meeting House, built in 1775.

**0.9**  **Traffic light. Bear left on Route 49 (sign for Quinton).**

**3.5**  **Cross Quinton's Bridge.**

If you look to the left before crossing the bridge, you will see the Weatherby House, which sits back from the road (private residence). A marker explains its significance in the nearby skirmish.

Quinton's Bridge was the location of a Revolutionary War skirmish on March 18, 1778. A British and American Loyalist force raided Salem County in a foraging expedition and as retaliation for county farmers' supplying Washington's Army during that famous winter at Valley Forge. Seven colonials were killed defending the bridge.

In the 1860s, the Quinton Glassworks produced 3 million square feet of fine plate glass annually.

**3.6**  **Traffic light. Left on Route 581 (Alloway Road).**

There are some small hills on this road. You enter Alloway at 6.0 miles. A good place to stop is the Old Alloway Merchandise Store. The store features a collection of old fashioned candy and local crafts.

**6.4**  **Traffic Light. Right on Route 540 (Telegraph Road).**

In 1739 Caspar Wistar imported four Rotterdam glassblowers and started the first glass factory in America. It was located about one mile north of this intersection. Unfortunately, there are no remains of this important industrial site.

**6.6**  **Left on Friesburg Road (sign for Bostwick Lake).**

Up until the early 1900s, this area of southeast Salem

County was considered an "island" of the Pine Barrens. Farms have altered the ecology, but there are still stretches of mixed hardwoood forests and Pitch Pines to be seen.[8]

There are small hills along this road. You'll pedal past the Holly Hills Golf Course at 9.6 miles.

**10.7 Stop. Right on Route 635 (Cohansey Road).**

This pavement is rough in sections. There are large farms on both sides of the road.

**12.4 Flashing yellow light. Right on Route 540 (Cohansey-Harmersville Road).**

The Cohansey General Store is a good place to stop for a break.

**14.2 Stop. Straight at intersection with Marlboro Road, now on Route 667.**

**15.4 Stop. Continue straight at intersection with Route 49, still on Route 667.**

**17.5 Left on Jericho Road (unmarked). Sign for Quinton Sportsmans Club.**

Note the pine woods along this road.

**20.3 Right on Hell Neck Road.**

**22.4 Stop. Right on Maskells Mill Road.**

The road goes through the Maskells Mill State Wildlife Area. There is a small bridge at Maskells Mill Pond at 23.2 miles.

**23.8 Left on Smick Road.**

The Lower Alloways Creek Historical Museum is on the left at 24.8 miles. It is open by special appointment. Call (609) 935-1938.

**25.2 Stop. Right on Route 623 (Harmersville-Canton Road).**

The Ye Olde Pumpkin Tavern c.1750 at 26.9 miles is now a private residence.

**27.5 Traffic light. Left on Route 658 (sign for Hancocks Bridge).**

The general store at this intersection is another good place to pick up snacks. As you continue, the Salem Nuclear Plant is visible to the left.

**28.1 Stop. Left on Route 658.**

**28.4 Traffic light. Right on Locust Island Road.**

**28.5 Left on Buttonwood Road.**

**28.8 Right on Main Street.**

The Friends Meeting House at this intersection dates from 1756.

**30.0 Right on New Street.**

**30.5 Stop. Left on Locust Island Road.**

The Hancock House is located on the left at this intersection in Hancocks Bridge. At 5 A.M. on March 21, 1778, part of the same British and Tory force that had skirmished at Quinton's Bridge on March 18th, bayoneted 30 colonials (mostly Quakers) whom they had trapped in the house. Historical markers describe the house and the massacre. The house was built in 1734 by Judge William Hancock who was one of the victims.

**30.5 Cross Hancock's Bridge.**

**31.5 Left on 624 (Fort Elfsborg-Hancock's Bridge Road).**

There are views to the left across Abbot's Meadow toward the Delaware River.

**33.5 Right on Route 627 (Samwellbury Road).**

**33.7 Left on Fort Elfsborg Road.**

**35.1 Right on Route 625 (Fort Elfsborg Road).**

The historical marker describes nearby Fort Elfsborg. Under the direction of Swedish Governor Printz, Fort Elfsborg was established on the Delaware River in the 1640s. It was nicknamed Myggenborg (Mosquito castle) because of its inhospitable location. Despite the energetic leadership of the 400-lb. Printz, whom the local Indians called "large stomach", the fort and settlements upriver soon collapsed.[9]

**37.1 Continue through flashing yellow light.**

**37.8 Bear right, stay on Route 625, now Chestnut Street.**

**38.4 Stop. Left on Broadway.**

**38.5 Old Oak Tree and Friends Burial Ground on right.
End of tour.**

The Hancock House has one of the most intricate patterned brick walls in New Jersey.

**Edwin B. Forsythe National Wildlife Refuge at dawn.**

Janine A. Fisher

# Atlantic, Burlington, Camden and Gloucester Counties

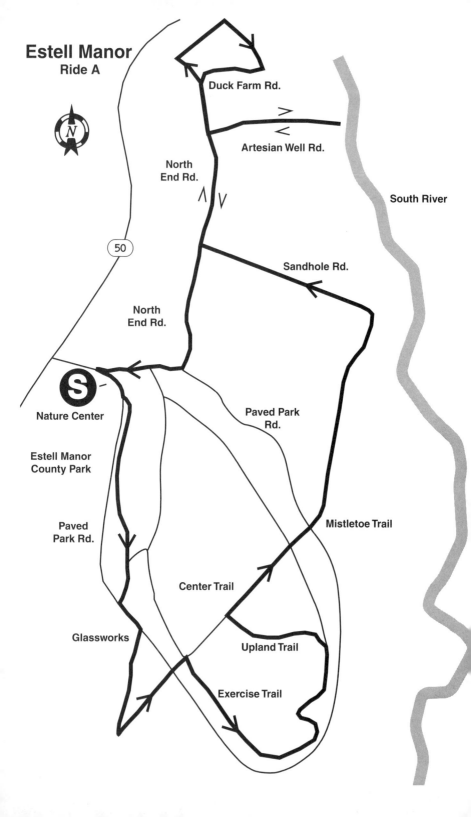

# Estell Manor
### Ride A

N

Duck Farm Rd.

Artesian Well Rd.

North
End Rd.

South River

50

Sandhole Rd.

North
End Rd.

S

Nature Center

Paved Park
Rd.

Estell Manor
County Park

Paved
Park Rd.

Mistletoe Trail

Center Trail

Upland Trail

Glassworks

Exercise Trail

# Estell Manor

## Start:

Estell Manor County Park, Estellville, Atlantic County. Estell Manor County Park is located on Route 50, 3.3 miles south of Mays Landing. Turn east into park entrance and continue to parking adjacent to nature center.

## Rides:

**Ride A** has two options, 3.6 or 8.7 miles both on dirt/sand trails.

**Ride B** is 25.1 miles on paved and dirt roads with light to moderate traffic.

Folklore is as much a part of the Pine Barrens as are fire, sand, cedar water and even the Pitch Pines. By far, the most famous legend is the Jersey Devil. Accounts vary, but most place the creature's birth in 1735. The cursed offspring of a woman named Leeds or Shrouds, it has been variously described, usually as having wings, with hooves, horns, a tail and the facial features of a horse or dog.

The three most common locations cited for the monster's birthplace are Leeds Point, Burlington and Estellville, somewhere near the location of present day Estell Manor County Park. The Estellville account is that a Mrs. Leeds found out she was pregnant with her thirteenth child and shouted "I hope it's the devil". Be careful what you wish for. She exiled the child from her home and it has been haunting the area ever since. During the last three centuries, there have been eyewitness sightings in the Pine Barrens and throughout New Jersey including Burlington, Bordentown, Haddonfield and Bridgeton. The creature has been accused of stealing livestock, killing dogs and generally terrorizing the populace. Believe what you want, but I'd keep my eyes open on these rides.[10]

Estell Manor Park contains 1,672 acres of mixed pine-hardwood forest and wetlands bordering the South and Great Egg Harbor Rivers. Within the park are the remains of two earlier industrial enterprises: the Estellville

Glassworks and the Bethlehem Loading Company. Ride A, which has two options, goes entirely within the park's border along trails and dirt/sand roads past some of these remains. Ride B leaves the park and goes through the wetlands of the nearby Lester G. MacNamara Wildlife Management Area. It returns through Corbin City, Peaslee Wildlife Management Area and Dorothy.

The nature center is a good place to learn about the area's history and ecology. Trail maps are available, but be advised that many of the older trails and roads are now heavily overgrown with brush and not good for bicycling. You can get specific information from Estell Manor County Park at (609) 625-7000.

## Directions: Ride A

**0.0** **Exit parking area to right. Turn immediately right on paved trail.**

**0.1** **Bear left across small bridge (trail is dirt at this point).**

Numbered stakes along this trail correspond to the "Nature Trail Guide" available at the nature center. Red numbers on trees correspond to "Common Trees of the Park Guide," also available from the nature center.

**0.1** **Bear right at fork (sign for picnic area).**

**0.4** **Turn right through picnic area after intersection with Laurel Trail and Pond Trail.**

**0.5** **Turn left along paved park road.**

**0.6** **Turn right on path through Estellville Glassworks ruins. Proceed onto sand trail.**

Take a break and learn about this important pinelands industry. Estellville Glassworks operated from 1825-1877. At the height of production it employed 80 men and boys. The factory chiefly produced plate glass for windows. These are reportedly the most extant 19th-century glass house ruins left in the state of New Jersey. The unique construction of native sandstone and brick arches contributed to the factory's durability.

Historical markers describe the various factory activities. The ruins include the melting furnace, pot house and flattening house. The site has been nominated for the

National Historic Register.

**0.8  Observation deck. Turn around and bear right at fork.**

This is an excellent waterfowl observation area. Look for Kingfishers *(Megaceryle halcyon)* perched on branches above the waterway. With their grayish-blue crest they are unmistakable. Stephen's Creek is a tributary of the Great Egg Harbor River.

**1.0  Stop. Continue straight across paved park road.**

**1.0  Right on Exercise Trail (unmarked).**

Watch for other cyclists and joggers using the exercise stations along this forest-lined trail.

**1.3  Trail bends sharply to left.**

**1.7  Bear to left, still on wider Exercise Trail.**

You are now paralleling the pavement to the right.

**1.8  Left on Upland Trail (unmarked).**

This trail goes through a thick growth of Mountain Laurel *(Kalmia latifolia)* that blooms from late May through early June.

**2.1  Right on Center Trail (unmarked).**

Marker 16 indicates a large oak that was once in a more open area when much of this forest was cleared.

At 2.2 miles is the intersection with Laurel Trail. At 2.2 miles continue across the narrow bridge through swamp area. Use caution, it can be slippery when wet. Look for growth of sphaghnum moss and Highbush Blueberry *(Vaccinium corymbosum)* in this swamp.

**2.4  Continue straight across excercise trail and paved road onto Mistletoe Trail.**

This section of trail can be very wet.

**2.7  Left at sign for footbridge. Go immediately across footbridge.**

**2.8  Left at T intersection on Sandhole Road (unmarked).**

**3.3  Intersection with North End Road. If you turn left and bear right through the gate onto the paved road, the nature center will be on the left at 3.6 miles. For a longer ride turn right.**

North end road can be very wet in sections.

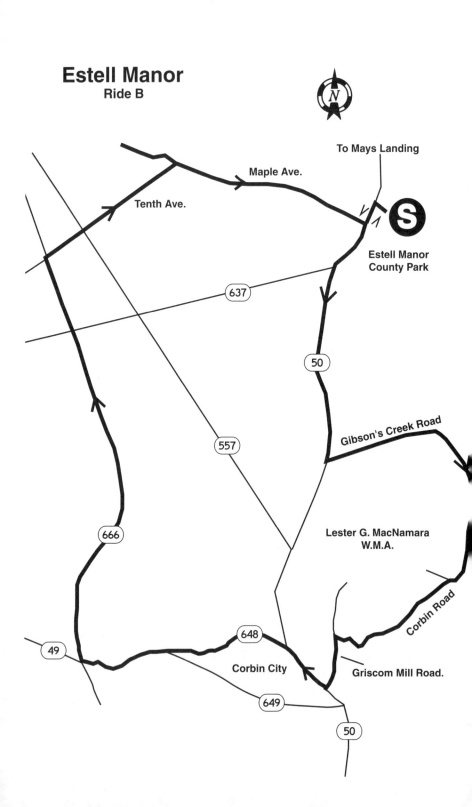

# Estell Manor
## Ride B

To Mays Landing

Maple Ave.

Tenth Ave.

Estell Manor
County Park

S

637

50

557

Gibson's Creek Road

666

Lester G. MacNamara
W.M.A.

Corbin Road

648

49

Corbin City

Griscom Mill Road.

649

50

At 3.5 miles there are a series of historical markers describing the Bethlehem Loading Company. Only the foundations of a few factory buildings still exist.

With the advent of World War I 10,000 acres of Pine Barrens was turned into an enormous munitions plant complex. Over 80 factory buildings were constructed and an entire town north of the park known as Belcoville was built to house workers. When production ceased in 1919, the plant had manufactured thousands of shells for the war. During World War II the remaining buildings and rail tracks were removed for scrap steel and iron. Today, only a few foundations and some rail beds remain amidst the regrown forest.

**4.1 Right on Artesian Well Road (unmarked). Road just after gate.**

**4.6 End of Artesian Well Road. Turn around.**

An old well sits at this intersection; its water unfortunately is unsafe for drinking. To the left is a boat launch ramp for South River which offers a quiet place for a ride break. A little way to the right is the Smith-Ireland Cemetery.

**5.1 Right on North End Road through gate.**

**5.2 Right on Duck Farm Road.**

Many of the roads and corresponding tree numbers date from 40 years ago when the park was a private hunting area.

**5.7 Left at tree # 200 (sign on large oak to right) on unmarked trail.**

**6.1 Bear right at fork (unmarked).**

Portions of this trail are the remains of an old railbed.

**6.7 Right on unmarked trail.**

The South River is visible to the left along this trail.

**7.1 Right on Duck Farm Road (unmarked). Continue back on Duck Farm Road to intersection with North End Road.**

Tree with # 200 marker is on the left at 7.2 miles.

**7.6 Left on North End Road. Continue through gates back toward main park area, still on North End Road.**

**8.5 Bear right at gate onto paved road.**

**8.7 Nature center on left. End of tour.**

# Directions: Ride B

**0.0  Exit parking toward Route 50. Turn left on Route 50.**

At 0.3 mile Stephen's Lake is on the right.

**3.5  Left on Gibson's Creek Road (dirt).**

This road leads into the Lester G. MacNamara Wildlife Management Area, a pristine area containing 13,337 acres of mostly wetlands between the Tuckahoe and Great Egg Harbor rivers. It is the oldest wildlife management area in the state, land acquisition having started in 1937.

**5.2  Gibson's Creek Road bends to right and becomes Griscom Road (unmarked).**

Gibson's Creek, which flows into the Great Egg Harbor River is to the left. The pond to the right is an excellent place for bird watching. Some Mute Swans *(Cygnus olor)* have become almost year-round residents in this area. In summer look for blooming White Water-lily *(Nymphaea odorata).*

**7.5  Left on Corbin Road (unmarked).**

Continue through wetlands area and take in the great view across the wetlands to the left toward Middle River and Great Egg Harbor.

**9.4  Road bends sharply to the left, becomes Griscom Mill Road (paved at 9.8 miles).**

**10.2 Stop. Right on Route 50 north.**

This is Corbin City. On the left just after the turn is the Corbin Cafe.

**10.8 Left on Route 648 (Buck Hill Road).**

At 11.0 miles use caution at railroad crossing.

**12.2 Bear right onto Route 649 (Head of River Road).**

At 13.0 there is a pond to the right as you enter the 14,000 acre Peaslee Wildlife Management Area.

**14.0 Right on Route 666 (Cape May Ave). Last turn before intersection with Route 49.**

Is it just a coincidence that Route 666 is near the birthplace of the Jersey Devil? The road continues through the wildlife management area before entering an area of development at 17.7 miles.

**18.8 Flashing yellow light. Continue straight at intersection**

**with Route 637, still on Route 666.**

Enter the town of Dorothy and continue past houses.

**19.9 Right on Tenth Ave.**

**20.5 Stop. Continue straight across Route 557 (Tuckahoe Road), still on Tenth Avenue. Use caution crossing railroad tracks.**

**21.0 Stop. Continue straight across Estell Ave.,still on Tenth Ave.**

**22.1 Stop. Right on Maple Ave (unmarked). Pavement is a little rough.**

At 23.1 is Maple Lake Wildlife Management Area, a pleasant place to stop before finishing the last few miles of the ride.

At 24.8 miles you pass Estellville M.E. Church built in 1834 on land owned by John Estell. The church congregation consisted primarily of workers from the nearby Estellville Glassworks.

**24.9 Stop. Left on Route 50.**

**25.1 Right into Estell Manor Park. End of tour.**

**The simple architectural style of the Estellville M.E. Church makes it one of the prettiest churches in the Pine Barrens.**

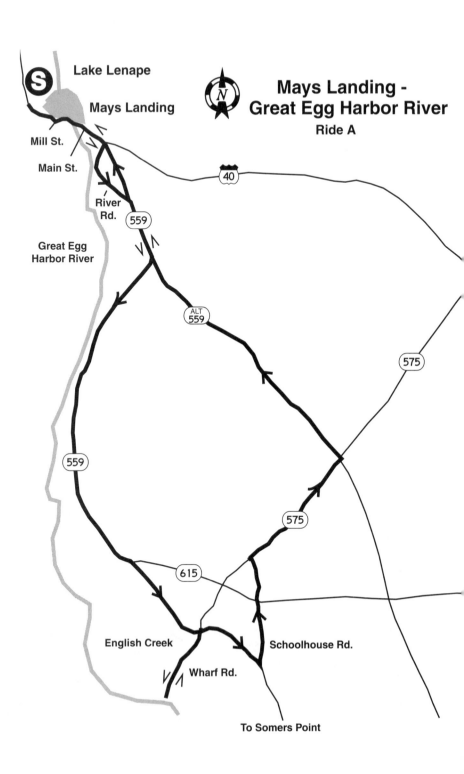

Lake Lenape

**S**

Mays Landing

Mill St.

Main St.

River
Rd.

**N**

# Mays Landing -
# Great Egg Harbor River
### Ride A

**40**

**559**

ALT
**559**

Great Egg
Harbor River

**575**

**559**

**575**

**615**

English Creek

Schoolhouse Rd.

Wharf Rd.

To Somers Point

# Mays Landing - Great Egg Harbor River

## Start:

Lake Lenape Park, Mays Landing, Atlantic County. Route 40 to Route 606 (Old Harding Highway) or Main Street. Follow signs to park entrance. Parking is available adjacent to Lake Lenape.

## Rides:

**Ride A** is 21.7 miles on paved roads (2.2 mile optional section on dirt) with moderate traffic.

**Ride B** is 37.8 miles on paved roads with moderate traffic (short section of heavy traffic on Route 40).

Combined with the nearby Tuckahoe River, the Great Egg Harbor River forms one of the five major Pine Barrens watersheds. Originating in Camden County, it flows southeast through the entire length of Atlantic County, culminating in Great Egg Harbor Bay west of Ocean City. Its unique name came from Cornelius Jacobsen Mey, the Dutch explorer whose name was given to Cape May and Mays Landing. Sailing south from New Amsterdam in the small ship *Fortuyn*, he explored the bay (which he referred to as a large lake). Mey spotted large piles of shorebird eggs along the shore at the mouth of the river and called it Eyren Haven (Harbor of Eggs).

Early settlers established settlements at Catawba, English Creek and Mays Landing. During the Revolution the river was a haven for privateers who would offload their booty along the river. In addition to fishing and farming, early industry included shipbuilding and, in the 19th century, iron and glass manufacturing.

These two rides explore a large portion of this watershed from Penny Pot in the north to English Creek Landing in the south. Ride A goes through Mays Landing, south along the navigable portion of the river as it widens toward the bay. Ride B goes north through the pines past historic Weymouth Furnace, along one of the most popular canoeing routes in the Pine Barrens. It then continues through an area of large blueberry and produce farms.

Lake Lenape Park has restrooms, picnic and camping facilities. The rides can be easily combined at the park. The combined mileage is 59.5 miles. Call the Atlantic County Parks System at (609) 645-5960 for more information.

## Directions: Ride A

**0.0  Exit park to left on Route 559 south.**

Go through Wheaton Industries plant.

**0.2  Stop. Left on Mill Street. Cross over Great Egg Harbor River.**

**0.3  Right on Main Street.**

The Mill Street Pub is at 0.5 mile.

**0.7  Traffic light. Continue straight, now on Route 40. Use caution—moderate to heavy traffic.**

The Presbyterian Church was built in 1841. There are a few restaurants and shops along the ride through Mays Landing.

Gaskill County Park is to the right. This is the tidal head of the Great Egg Harbor River. In the summer, there are crowds of boaters enjoying these placid waters.

**1.0  Traffic light. Get in right lane and turn right on Route 559  (sign for Somers Point).**

**1.1  Right on River Road (road is just before Sugar Hill Inn).**

**2.1  Stop. Right on Route 559.**

**3.1  Bear to right at intersection with Alt. Route 559, still on Route 559 (Mays Landing-Somers Point Road).**

At 5.1 miles Great Egg Harbor River is visible to the right. Across the street is an historical marker describing the old Catawba Meeting House and Burial Ground.

Continue past the Green Tree Golf Course and through River Bend County Park. At 8.0 miles the road crosses Powell Creek.

**8.3  Bear right, at intersection with Route 615, still on Route 559. Sign for Somers Point and Ocean City.**

At 9.6 miles a bridge crosses English Creek.

(At 9.8 miles you can take an optional 2.2 mile side trip by turning right on Wharf Road, which turns to dirt. Go 1.1 miles to the end of the road.)

At the end of the road is a small marina and a great view of the Great Egg Harbor River across English Creek. Across the river is the Lester G. Macnamara Wildlife Management Area, a good place to look for Great Blue Herons *(Ardea herodias).*

**11.0 Left on Schoolhouse Road.**

**12.0 Stop. Left on Route 615 (Zion Road) and immediate right, back on Schoolhouse Road.**

**12.5 Stop. Right on Route 575 (English Creek Avenue).**

There are a series of small hills on this road.

**14.6 Traffic light. Left on Alt. Route 559.**

**18.3 Bear right at intersection with Thelma Avenue, still on Alt. Route 559.**

**18.8 Stop. Right on Route 559.**

**20.6 Flashing red light. Left on Route 559 (Atlantic Avenue).**

**20.7 Traffic light. Get in center lane and proceed onto Route 40 west.**

Reenter Mays Landing.

**21.1 Traffic light. Continue straight, now on Main Street.**

**21.4 Bear left on Mill Street.**

**21.5 Right, at flashing yellow light, on 559 north. (sign for Lake Lenape).**

**21.7 Right at park entrance. End of tour.**

## *Directions: Ride B*

**0.0 Exit park to right on Route 559 north.**

**0.2 Right, still on Route 559 north.**

Lake Lenape County Park is on the right. The county started acquiring land in 1978 and this is now the largest park in the county system with 1,900 acres. At 3.0 miles is the entrance to the Acagisca group camping area.

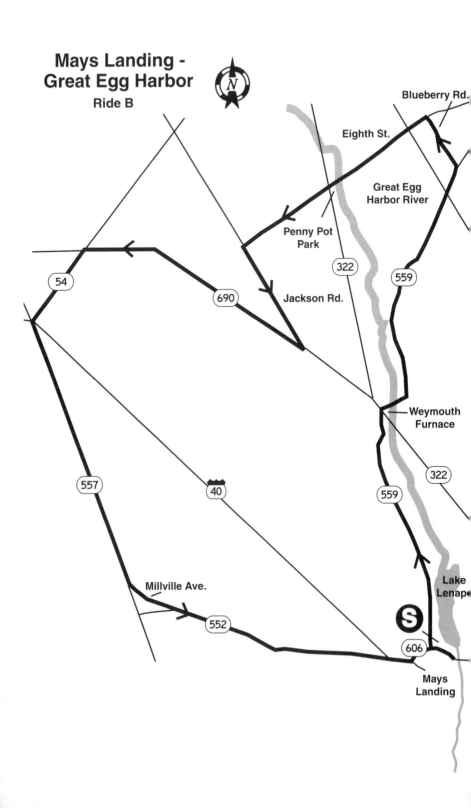

# Mays Landing -
# Great Egg Harbor
## Ride B

Blueberry Rd.

Eighth St.

Great Egg
Harbor River

Penny Pot
Park

54

690

322

559

Jackson Rd.

Weymouth
Furnace

557

40

322

559

Lake
Lenape

Millville Ave.

552

S

606

Mays
Landing

**5.1 Traffic light. Continue straight across Route 322, still on Route 559.**

At 5.4 miles on the right is Weymouth Furnace County Park. This small park (about eight acres) is the former location of the Weymouth Iron Furnace and Papermill. A large iron furnace and forge operated here from 1802-1865. The forge produced munitions for the War of 1812. Much of the 900 tons of castings produced annually were used as the original water pipe for Philadelphia. A railway was built to Mays Landing where goods could be offloaded to be transported by ship to various cities along the east coast.[11]

After the iron forge ceased production in 1862 two papermills operated here. In an early example of recycling, these papermills initially used old rope, rags and bagging for paper manufacturing, before later switching to wood pulp. They ceased operation in 1887. Today only a few interesting ruins of either enterprise remain.

**5.6 Bear left, still on 559 north, at intersection with Route 623.**

This road goes through one of the major blueberry production areas in the state. Many of the state's 8,000 acres are located around Hammonton. New Jersey is ranked second

**Weymouth Forge contains some of the most interesting ruins in Atlantic County.** Janine A. Fisher

93

in production of blueberries in the United States. These long rows of plants bloom in May and the fruit ripens in late June. At 7.7 miles is the Atlantic Blueberry Headquarters.

At 10.0 miles the road goes over the Atlantic City Expressway.

**10.5 Left, still on Route 559 north. (Blueberry Road).**

More blueberry fields border this road.

**11.6 Flashing Yellow light. Left on Eighth St.**

At 11.9 miles the road goes over the Atlantic City Expressway. This road, with a pine forest on each side, goes through Folsom.

At 13.4 miles there is a small wooden bridge over Penny Pot Stream.

**13.7 Penny Pot Park is to the left after crossing the bridge over Great Egg Harbor River.**

Penny Pot Park is a popular put-in spot for canoeists. The trip from here to Lake Lenape takes about seven hours. The dam is said to be one of the most expensive per square foot in the country. It was built from teakwood salvaged from old ships. There are picnic benches here and this is a relaxing spot for a ride break.

**13.9 Stop. Straight across Route 561.**

**14.0 Traffic light. Continue straight across Route 322, still on Eighth Street.**

At 14.1 miles cross the narrow bridge at Penny Pot Lake. Sections of pavement get rough along this road.

**16.1 Stop. Left on Jackson Road.**

This road also has rough pavement.

**18.5 Stop. Right on Route 690 (Weymouth-Malaga Road).**

Cross railroad tracks at 22.3 miles.

**23.6 Traffic light. Left on Route 54. Use caution, there is moderate, high-speed traffic. Use the wide shoulder.**

At 23.7 miles is the 54 Diner.

**25.2 Traffic light. Left on Route 40. Use caution, there is moderate high-speed traffic.**

There is a convenience store at this intersection.

**25.4 Traffic light. Right on Route 557.**

**25.5 Left, still on Route 557.**

As you continue southeast you pass a number of fruit and vegetable markets including Bertuzzi's and Al's. There is a custard stand at the Five Points intersection.

**31.1 Left on Millville Ave.**

Cross railroad tracks at 31.2 miles.

**31.8 Stop. Left on Route 552 (Bear's Head Road).**

Use caution—moderate high-speed traffic. At 34.4 miles the road bends left, then right as it crosses the South River.

**36.6 Stop. Straight on Route 40. Use caution—heavy traffic.**

**37.1 Traffic light. Left on Route 606 (Old Harding Highway). Use caution.**

Located about one mile south (right) of this intersection was Walker's Forge. Also named Monroe Forge, it operated from 1816–1853. No reminder exists, except the name of the housing development.

**37.6 Straight on Route 559 south.**

**37.8 Left into park entrance. End of tour.**

**A scenic vista near Smithville, Atlantic County.**

Janine A. Fisher

95

# Edwin Forsythe -
# Port Republic
### Ride A

9

Great Creek
Rd.

Wildlife Drive

West Pool

Noyes
Museum

**S**

Headquarters

Observation Tower

Dike

East Pool

Turtle Cove

N

# Edwin B. Forsythe - Port Republic

## Start:

Edwin B. Forsythe National Wildlife Refuge, Oceanville, Atlantic County. Route 9 to sign for Edwin B. Forsythe National Wildlife Refuge. Turn at Great Creek Road to parking near visitor center. Parking is free, but there is a fee for admittance to the driving loop.

## Rides:

**Ride A** is 7.8 miles on dirt park road with light to moderate traffic (watch for stopped cars).

**Ride B** is 37.4 miles on paved roads with light to moderate traffic. Combining the two rides results in a 45.2 mile ride.

The National Wildlife Refuge System is an important, yet often overlooked, part of America's public lands. Nationwide, there are over 500 units under the control of the U.S. Fish and Wildlife Service. Habitat is maintained to increase and protect diverse wildlife populations.

One of the most important units in the Mid-Atlantic area is the Edwin B. Forsythe Refuge. Located on the Atlantic flyway, this refuge contains over 40,000 acres of wetlands, barrier beaches, tidal pools and Pine Barren uplands in two separate divisions: Brigantine and Barnegat. This diverse ecosystem attracts almost 300 migratory and year-round bird species, some of which are endangered and threatened. The refuge is named for the New Jersey congressman who was active in Pine Barrens and other environmental legislation.

The first ride follows the refuge's driving loop past tidal pools and coastal wetlands. This is a simple, well-known ride popular with locals and tourists alike. Before starting, pick up driving loop and birding guides at the entrance kiosk.[12] It's a good idea to bring binoculars for birding. If you are riding in warm weather, bring insect repellent. The second ride leaves the refuge and goes through eastern Atlantic County. It is an area of wetlands, forest, farms, old towns and recent residential development. There are interesting side trips to Oyster Creek, the Chestnut Neck Memorial and the Renault Winery.

Before or after your ride make sure to visit the Noyes Museum, which is located a short distance from the parking area. The museum has one of the largest collections of decoys in the country and a number of different art exhibits throughout the year. There is a small admittance fee. Call (609) 652-8848 for more information.

## Directions: Ride A

**0.0    Exit parking past entrance kiosk. Bear left at wildlife drive sign on Great Neck Road.**

This one-way road loops around the refuge and returns toward the parking area. The Leeds Walking Trail is to the right (no bikes).

At 0.1 mile on left is a road to the gull tower and gull pond.

To the left is the West Pool. This 900-acre pond was created to attract birds which need freshwater for drinking and bathing. At 1.1 miles is an observation tower. The tower gives you a good view of both the West and East pools. The East Pool is brackish, a mixture of salt and fresh water. Water levels in this pond are contolled to encourage the growth of various plants.

On the right is Turtle Cove, a tidal marsh leading into Reeds Bay. Look for Great Blue Herons *(Ardea herodias)*, Snowy Egrets *(Egretta thula)*, and even an occasional Glossy Ibis *(Plegadis falcinellus)* along both sides of this road. Brant *(Branta bernicla)*, one of the refuge's most important species, often seem to be feeding here. In fact, they are picking up sand for their gizzards. Brant are identified by a full black breast and a small fleck of white on the neck.

In the distance is the Atlantic City skyline and Brigantine. Although only a few miles away, the casinos and hotels of Atlantic City seem to be of another world.

**2.6    Road bends to left.**

The islands to the right are part of this refuge and the Absecon Wildlife Management Area, which is managed by the New Jersey Division of Fish, Game and Wildlife.

Occasionally there are Black-bellied Plovers *(Pluvialis squatarola)* feeding on the mud flats on the edge of the dike. In summer they do indeed have a distinctive black belly.

**3.3  Road bends to left, now on Monroe's Swamp Road.**

You can often spot American Black Ducks *(Anas rubripes)* in the pond. Look for a metallic violet wing patch.

**5.8  Road angles left.**

**6.1  Road bends left.**

This area of upland forest, which is essentially the edge of the Pine Barrens, attracts different bird species. Refuge managers use controlled burning and mowing to encourage certain plant growth.

**7.5  Left on Park Road (unmarked/ paved).**

**7.8  Edwin B. Forsythe parking. End of tour.**

## *Directions: Ride B*

**0.0  Exit parking on Great Creek Road toward Route 9.**

If you bear left on Lily Lake Road, you will come to the Noyes Museum in a short distance.

Lily Lake is on the left.

**0.7  Traffic light. Right on Route 9.**

**0.8  Right on Route 618 (Leeds Point Road).**

This road goes past the Leeds Point Post Office.

**2.8  Stop. Right on Alt. 561 (Moss Mill Road).**

**3.1  Bear to left, Alt. 561 is now called Oyster Creek Road.**

This road reenters the Edwin B. Forsythe Wildlife Management Area. On the right is Scott's Landing Road.

**4.2  End of road. Turn around.**

Oyster Creek leads into Great Bay. The Oyster Creek Inn is a good place to stop to fill up on tasty local seafood and bay atmosphere. It's easy to spend an afternoon just watching the well-worn working boats coming in with their catch. Call (609) 652-9871 for hours and reservations.

**5.6  Continue straight at intersection with Leeds Point Road, still on Alt. 561 (Moss Mill Road).**

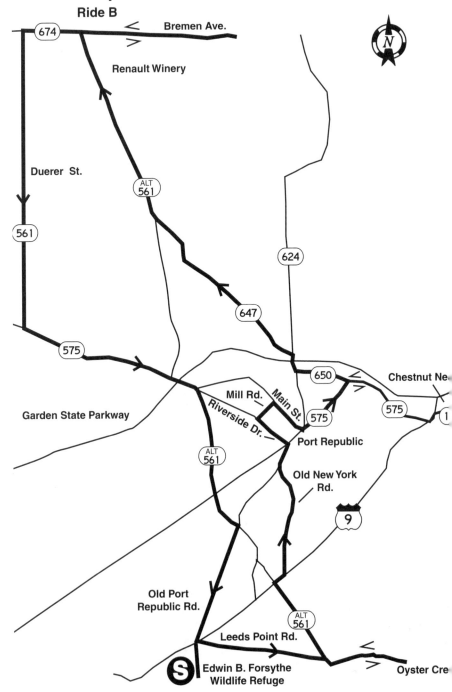

# Edwin Forsythe -
# Port Republic
## Ride B

Bremen Ave.

674

Renault Winery

Duerer St.

ALT 561

561

624

575

647

650

Chestnut Ne

Mill Rd.

Main St.

Riverside Dr.

575

575

1

Garden State Parkway

ALT 561

Port Republic

Old New York Rd.

9

N

Old Port Republic Rd.

ALT 561

Leeds Point Rd.

**S** Edwin B. Forsythe Wildlife Refuge

Oyster Cre

**6.9 Traffic light. Right on Route 9.**

Smithville Village has shops and restaurants located in a number of restored 18th- and 19th-century buildings. The village is located at the former location of an 18th-century stagecoach stop.

**7.1 Left on Route 610 (Old New York Road).**

**9.1 Left on Riverside Drive (Turn before Nacote Creek Bridge**

In the last few years, bridges over various Pine Barrens streams have become crowded in spring with fishermen netting American Eels *(Anguilla rostrata)*. The eels, which are the only catradomous fish on the east coast, are returning to the local fresh and brackish water after being spawned at sea. The elvers (small eels) are captured and sold live to European and Asian exporters who raise them to maturity for consumption. In 1996 these elvers were bringing up to $350 per pound! The state is considering placing restrictions on this harvest.

**9.8 Right on Mill Road.**

Mill Pond (left) and Nacote Creek (right) are both good bird watching spots.

Port Republic is one of the most picturesque towns in Atlantic County. Many buildings date from the 19th century. Historical markers describe the significance of some of them.

**10.1 Right on Route 575 (Main Street).**

**10.7 Stop. Left on Route 575 (Old New York Road).**

**11.7 Stop. Right on Route 575 (Chestnut Neck Road).**

As you leave town the Port Republic Wildlife Management Area is to the left.

**13.1 Stop. Left on Route 9.**

**13.2 Right on Route 167 (Old New York Road). Unmarked. Turn around; return on Route 575 toward Port Republic.**

The Chestnut Neck Memorial is on the left as soon as you cross Route 9. This almost hidden memorial commemorates the village of Chestnut Neck, which was destroyed in the Revolutionary War.

During the war Chestnut Neck was an important privateering center. In 1778 it was the largest seacoast village between Sandy Hook and Cape May. There were a dozen houses, an inn and tavern and a ship landing. Privateers would bring captured ships here, where their wares could be offloaded and auctioned to aid the colonial war cause.

On September 30, 1778 the British launched an attack against the area from Staten Island. It was a major force with a number of ships, including the armed sloops H.M.S. *Zebra*, H.M.S. *Nautilus*, and H.M.S. *Greenwich*, and almost 400 troops. Though the harbor was difficult to navigate, a few transports were able to get near the village and put troops ashore. The colonists were able to erect a small fort, but it was overrun and the village was burned to the ground on October 6, 1778. The village was located near the Mullica River. (If you continue down the road till it turns to dirt, you'll see where the village was located — near where the marina is today).

Attempts by the British to get further upstream and destroy other privateering centers and the ironworks at Batsto were unsuccessful. Except for an attack on Pulaskis Legion a few days later (see Tuckerton section), the British incursion into this part of the New Jersey coast was over for the remainder of the war.[13]

**15.9 Continue straight at intersection with Route 575 (Old New York Road), now on Route 650.**

**16.8 Right on Route 624 (Clarks Landing Road).**

You immediately go under the Garden State Parkway.

The Port Republic General Store is a good place to stop for food and drinks.

**17.0 Left on Route 647 (Port Republic Road). This becomes Cologne-Port Republic Road. Follow signs for Route 647 as road bends to right then left.**

This road goes through an area of farms and residential development.

**19.9 Bear right on Alt. Route 561 (Moss Mill Road).**

**23.0 Right on Bremen Avenue (if you want to visit Renault Winery).**

**23.6 Renault Winery on right. Turn around on Bremen Avenue.**

Renault Winery was founded in 1864. Call (609) 965-2111 for more information about the winery, various events and to make dining reservations. The Wine Garden Cafe is a great place for a casual lunch. Though the wine may tempt you, you'd be wise to save the drinking until you get home; there's still a lot of riding ahead of you.

**24.2 Stop. Continue straight across intersection with Alt. Route 561, still on Bremen Avenue.**

Egg Harbor City was founded in 1854 by German immigrants who purchased 30,000 acres. They laid out a city whose street names, such as Berlin, Frankfurt and Leipzig, came from their native country.

**25.0 Stop. Left on Route 561 (Duerer Street).**

This area of the Pine Barrens west of Atlantic City was mostly excluded from protection in Pinelands legislation and is becoming largely developed.

**26.8 Four-way stop. Continue straight at intersection with Cologne Avenue, still on Route 561.**

**29.5 Four-way stop. Left on Route 575 (Pomona-Port Republic Road).**

Stockton College is on the right along this road. It was named for Richard Stockton, signer of the Declaration of Independence.

The road crosses the Garden State Parkway at 32.2 miles.

**32.6 Right on Alt. Route 561 (Moss Mill Road).**

**34.1 Flashing red light. Continue straight at intersection with Pitney Road, still on Alt. Route 561.**

**34.8 Right on Old Port Republic Road.**

This road goes through an area of woods and recent residential development.

**36.6 Stop. Right on Route 9.**

**36.7 Traffic light. Left on Great Creek Road.**

**37.4 Edwin B. Forsythe parking. End of tour.**

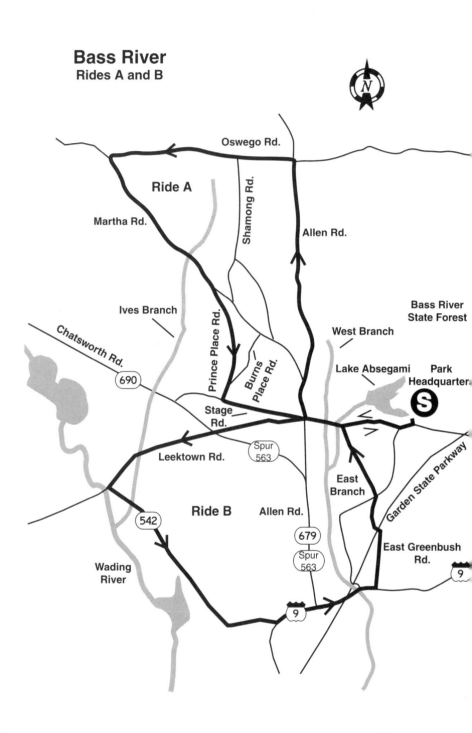

**Bass River**
Rides A and B

# Bass River

## Start:

Bass River State Forest, Burlington County. Garden State Parkway Exit 50 north to Route 9 north through New Gretna. Turn left on East Greenbush Road. Or from Exit 52 south turn right on East Greenbush Avenue. Turn right on Stage Road and follow signs to state forest headquarters on left. There is a fee for park admission and parking.

## Rides:

**Ride A** is 12.8 miles on paved, dirt/sand roads and narrow sugar sand roads with light traffic.

**Ride B** is 11.1 miles on paved roads with light to moderate traffic.

Most scientists agree with the seemingly contradictory statement that without fire the Pine Barrens would not exist. Many plants have developed resistance to fire and indeed seem to thrive after fires. The dominant tree of the area, the Pitch Pine *(Pinus rigida),* is a fascinating example of this evolutionary development. Its thick bark is able to protect it from heat and within a few weeks of a fire, while the ground is still smoldering, the tree sends forth new growth. Within a few months a tree may be covered in green. More important, the Pitch Pine's seeds are small and have a difficult time getting past ground debris into the sandy soil. Fire clears this duff and the seeds can become rooted, pushing out competing species, such as the Black Oak *(Quercus velutina).*

Before man came to the Pine Barrens all fires were started by lightning. This process of fire, renewal and evolution went unchecked, except by streams and other water barriers. However, with man this process has been altered. Some historians believe Native Americans burned the woods to improve hunting. Early settlers burned the understory to improve wild blueberry growth. In the 19th century, many accidental fires were started by iron furnaces, forges and charcoal burners.

In the 20th century, most fires have been started by carelessness and arson. Modern firefighting techniques have been applied to the Pine Barrens with varying success. Fires are fought with aerial chemical drops, large tanker trucks and other methods. In the state forests, fire strips are cleared and there is a policy of controlled burning. Despite these efforts dozens of fires occur in the Pine Barrens each year.

Foresters must strike a balance between control and the natural ecology of this unique area, which benefits from fire. These two rides go past the location of many fires that have occurred in the last hundred years. Ride A goes mostly through the state forest, while Ride B leaves the park to the Wading River and then crosses the Bass River at New Gretna. As it returns to the park it goes past a firefighters' memorial that is a sobering reminder of one of the costs of fire in the pines.

## Directions: Ride A

**0.0   Exit park headquarters to right on Stage Road.**

Bass River State Forest contains 18,208 non-contiguous acres in Burlington and Ocean Counties. The state started acquiring land in 1905. The park's centerpiece is Lake Absegami, where swimming is permitted in the summer. For information on camping and cabin rentals write or call the park headquarters. The address and phone number are listed in the appendix. There are public restrooms and a water fountain at the bathhouse next to Lake Absegami. Make sure to fill up on water before leaving the park.

**0.9   Stop. Continue straight, still on Stage Road.**

Cross small bridge over East Branch of the Bass River at 1.0 mile and bridge over West Branch of Bass River at 1.3 miles.

About a mile south of here the two branches join to form the Bass River which then flows south to the Mullica.

**1.4   Right on Allen Road. Road bends to right; continue past intersection with Martha Road (unmarked).**

The road goes over a small bridge that crosses Bartlett's Branch at 2.3 miles and leaves the state forest. There is a brief section of wetlands.

The road is roughly paved and becomes dirt/sand at 4.5 miles.

**4.5** **Left on Oswego Road (unmarked). This is the first crossroads. It is a sand road, with sections of heavy sugar sand.**

Believe it or not, this was an important 19th-century road, connecting Martha furnace with Munionfield and other small settlements to the east.

Look for the remains of some old buildings along this road.

**6.9** **Left on Martha Road (unmarked). This is a more narrow road than Oswego Road, only six feet wide in places.**

Calico, a small early 19th-century settlement was located near this intersection (nothing remains).

There are some more old ruins along Martha Road.

At 8.7 miles there is a pond to the left. Water can be fairly deep across the road as the pond flows into Ives Branch.

**9.0** **Bear right on Prince Place Road (unmarked). This is a wider road than Martha Road.**

Bracken Ferns *(Pterdium aquilinum)* are the most prevalent plant in the undergrowth along this narrow road.

**10.3** **Bear right at intersection with road on left, now on Burns Place Road (unmarked).**

**10.5** **Stop. Left on Stage Road (unmarked/paved).**

**11.6** **Stop. Continue straight at intersection with Route 679 (Allen Road), still on Stage Road.**

Continue across bridge over Bass River at 11.8 miles.

**11.9** **Bear left at sign for Bass River State Forest, still on Stage Road.**

**12.8** **Left at park entrance. End of tour.**


## Directions: Ride B

**0.0** **Exit park headquarters to right on Stage Road.**

**0.9** **Stop. Continue straight, still on Stage Road.**

Cross bridge over East Branch of Bass River at 1.0 mile and West Branch at 1.3 miles.

**1.3** **Left on Leektown Road.**

**2.4** **Stop. Continue straight at intersection with Chatsworth Road, still on Leektown Road (sign for Batsto).**

This crossroads called Leektown is marked by a small store at the intersection.

You cross a little bridge over Ives Branch at 3.4 miles and then the road bends to the left.

**4.0** **Stop. Left on Route 542.**

At this intersection is the scenic Wading River, an inviting place for a brief ride break. The Wading-Oswego and Batsto-Mullica river watershed is the largest watershed in the Pine Barrens.

At 4.4 miles you cross Ives Branch and go through a wetlands area. I saw a number of Red-winged Blackbirds (*Agelaius phoeniceus*) to the right at this spot. At 5.4 miles you cross a small bridge over Merrygold Branch as the river appears to the right.

**6.2** **Bear left, still on Route 542.**

**6.8** **Stop. Left on Route 9. Use caution—moderate to heavy traffic.**

There's a deli and restaurant in New Gretna.

**7.3** **Traffic light. Continue straight at Route 679 intersection, still on Route 9.**

**7.7** **Cross bridge over Bass River. Use caution, metal grid surface.**

Yacht building and marinas have been an important part of this area for a number of years.

**8.1** **Left on East Greenbush Road.**

At 8.6 miles the road crosses the bridge over the Garden State Parkway. Continue on East Greenbush Road as it bends right, then left. After you reenter Bass River State Forest look to the left for the Firefighters Memorial.

This memorial commemorates the firefighters who lost their lives in forest fires on May 25, 1936 and July 22, 1977.

**10.2** **Stop. Right on Stage Road.**

**11.1** **Left into park entrance. End of tour.**

A Pine Barrens road winds past a recently burned Pitch Pine forest.

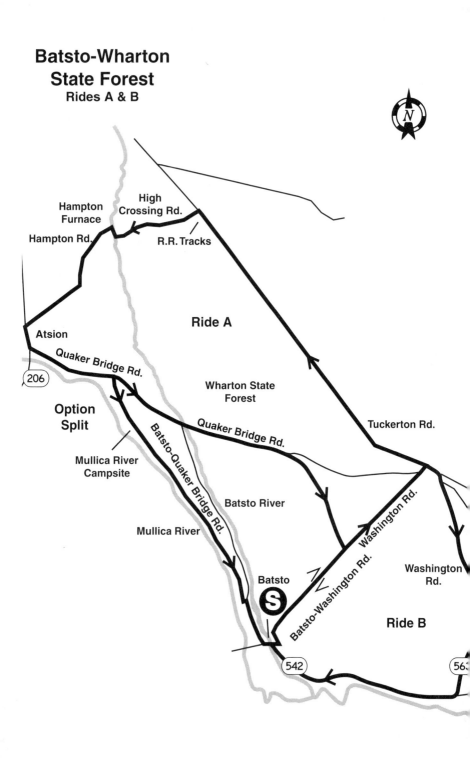

# Batsto-Wharton
# State Forest
## Rides A & B

Hampton
Furnace

High
Crossing Rd.

Hampton Rd.

R.R. Tracks

Ride A

Atsion

Quaker Bridge Rd.

206

Wharton State
Forest

Option
Split

Quaker Bridge Rd.

Tuckerton Rd.

Mullica River
Campsite

Batsto-Quaker Bridge Rd.

Batsto River

Washington Rd.

Mullica River

Batsto-Washington Rd.

Washington
Rd.

Batsto

S

Ride B

542

563

# Batsto-Wharton State Forest

## Start:

Batsto Visitor Center, Wharton State Forest, Burlington County. Atlantic City Expressway to Exit 28. Route 54 to Hammonton. Right on Route 542. Follow signs to Batsto Visitor Center on left.

## Rides:

**Ride A** is 28.1 or 27.2 miles on dirt/sand roads and forest trails with little traffic.

**Ride B** is 13.9 miles on dirt/sand roads, forest trails and paved roads with little traffic.

**Ride C** is 26.1 miles on paved roads with little to moderate traffic.

If you find yourself bicycling through the Pine Barrens during or after a rainstorm, strange as it may seem, think of iron. As the rain percolates through the vegetation and sand beneath your bike tires, it leaches various chemical compounds. The rain water becomes acidic enough to act upon iron salts found in the clay beds and banks of the Pine Barrens slow-moving streams. Iron compounds float to the surface of the streams and oxidize into a red sludge. Where streams are especially sluggish or shallow, this sludge combines with sand and can build up into a crust, resulting in what is known as bog iron.

In addition to bog iron, the Pine Barrens contained other materials necessary for the production of iron. These included wood for fuel, water to power the furnace bellows and sea shells, which were crushed to produce a necessary reagent. The first bog iron furnaces in the pines were started in the 1760s.

Charles Read started one of the most important at Batsto in 1766. Through subsequent owners Batsto grew and became an important supplier of munitions and other ironware to Washington's army during the Revolution. Batsto, like the dozens of other furnaces in the Pine Barrens, ceased production in the mid-19th century when cheaper fuel (coal) and higher-grade iron ore were discovered to the west.

These three rides connect Batsto with many surrounding historical sites, including those of other furnaces at Hampton and Atsion. Rides A and B go mostly through Wharton State Forest, through dense forest and past the location of once thriving towns. Ride C goes through the surrounding Atlantic and Burlington County countryside, returning through scenic Lower Bank along the Mullica River. Start your tour at the visitor center where you can obtain a map of Wharton State Forest and various plant and history guides. A walking tour of Batsto Village is highly recommended. For further information contact Wharton State Forest, Batsto headquarters at (609) 561-3262. Be aware that almost all sand/dirt roads in the forest are unmarked. Pay attention to mileage and landmarks to follow the directions.

## Directions: Ride A

**0.0  Exit parking to left on park entrance road.**

At 0.4 mile on the left is the Batsto forest service tower.

Wharton State Forest is named after Joseph Wharton, who owned Batsto and much of the surrounding area from 1873 to 1909. Wharton planned to sell the area's abundant water to Philadelphia and suburban New Jersey. When this scheme was thwarted by the New Jersey legislature, Wharton started large scale blueberry and lumber operations on his estate.

The state of New Jersey acquired 96,000 acres from Wharton's trustees in 1954. This land forms the core of Wharton State Forest's 110,273 acres, which form the state's largest contiguous public lands.

**0.9  Straight on Washington Road (unmarked/unpaved). This road becomes increasingly sandy, but stays fairly wide.**

**4.6  Left on Tuckerton Road (unmarked.) This is the second left at Washington intersection.**

The Tuckerton Road, one of the most important Pine Barrens roads, connected the populated area of Camden County with Tuckerton, where people traveled for religious meetings and in more recent years for shore vacations. The route splits just south of Medford into upper and lower routes and rejoined east of here for the rest of the way to Tuckerton. This is the upper or northern route.

It is narrower and has sections of heavy sugar sand. Continue past intersections with other roads and trails at 8.3 miles and 9.6 miles.

**11.6 Cross railroad tracks.**

**11.7 Left on High Crossing Road, immediately after crossing tracks (unmarked).**

This road goes through a lowlands area with small ponds and bogs. Look for Cinnamon Fern *(Osmunda cinnamomea)* in the area. Its distinctive fiddlehead shape is easy to spot in early spring.

**13.5 Cross small bridge with caution.**

Ruins of building visible to left at 13.8 miles.

**13.9 Cross small bridge over Batsto River. The road becomes**

**Visitors stroll by the Historic Wharton Mansion at Batsto Village.**

Janine A. Fisher

**113**

**progressively wider and sugar sand gives way to hardpacked dirt.**

Hampton Furnace was located here alongside the Batsto at this point. It produced tools, wagon axles and bar iron. Records indicate it ceased production around 1829.

There are wetlands to the right along the road. A small abandoned cranberry bog is on the right at 14.8 miles.

**15.3 Road bends to right.**

**15.4 Cross small bridge.**

**15.6 Cross small bridge.**

**17.1 Stop. Left at Route 206 (you can stay on the shoulder on the left a short distance, rather than crossing Route 206).**

Atsion was also started by Charles Read. Pig iron was brought here from Batsto, where it was converted into bar iron. More information on this area is contained in the Atsion section of this book. Public facilities are located adjacent to Atsion Lake across Route 206.

**17.4 Left on Quaker Bridge Road. Pavement soon ends and the surface becomes dirt/sand.**

Quaker Bridge Road was part of the southern or lower route of the Tuckerton Road.

**17.8 Cross railroad.**

You see the Mullica River to the right as you continue south.

## Option 1: Quaker Bridge route.

**19.4 Continue straight, at sign for Mullica River primitive camping, still on Quaker Bridge Road. Continue on main road.**

**21.3 Cross Quaker Bridge over the Batsto River. Stay on the main road after crossing bridge.**

In 1772 Quakers built a bridge here to cross the Batsto on the way to Tuckerton for their annual meeting. A small settlement grew up near the river.

In 1808 the Curly Grass Fern *(Schizaea pusilla)* was discovered here. Threatened and endangered, this unusual plant is one of the most well-known Pine Barrens plants.

The road continues through an upland area of mostly Pitch Pine. There are a few sections of heavy sugar sand.

114

**25.8** Stop. Right on Batsto-Washington Road (unmarked/dirt)

**27.2** Stop. Continue straight onto paved road (unmarked).

**28.1** Park entrance on right. End of tour.

## Option 2: Mullica River route

**19.4** Right at sign for Mullica River camping.

**20.0** Keep left on main path through camping areas.

This trail has sections of very heavy sugar sand.

**21.6** Left at sign for natural area (sign is straight ahead) on unnamed path.

**21.9** Bear right, continue on unnamed path.

**23.4** Bear right on Batsto-Quaker Bridge Road (unmarked). This is a wider road.

Batsto Lake will be on the left at 25.4 miles. It was created by damming the Batsto River to create power for the various enterprises at Batsto.

**26.6** Bear to right at Batsto Village fence.

**26.9** Stop. Left on Route 542 (paved).

**27.2** Entrance to Batsto Village. End of tour.

## Directions: Ride B

Follow directions for Ride A to 4.6 miles.

**4.6** Right on Tuckerton Road (unmarked).

**4.9** Right on Washington Road (unmarked).

Washington, an important crossroads village on the Tuckerton Road, was located a short distance from this intersection. A popular tavern operated here from 1775 through the 1850s.

**5.1** Continue straight at intersection with road on left, still on Washington Road.

This sand road has sections of large puddles, especially after rain.

**8.2** Left at large tree in center of road.

**8.5** Stop. Right on Route 563.

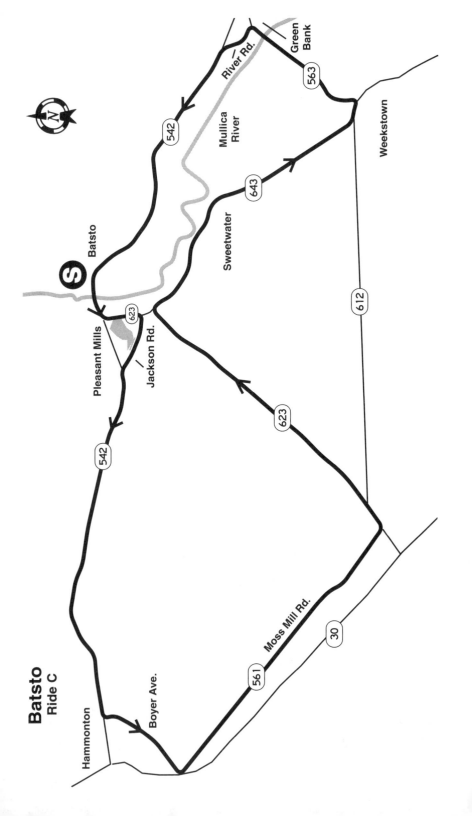

# Batsto
## Ride C

N

Hammonton

Boyer Ave.

542

Pleasant Mills

623

Jackson Rd.

S

Batsto

542

River Rd.

Green Bank

563

Weekstown

Mullica River

643

Sweetwater

623

612

561

Moss Mill Rd.

30

**9.7   Stop. Right on Route 542.**

Hermann City was located at 10.5 miles along the Mullica. This "city" had a major glass factory, dozens of workers' houses, a store and hotel. It was constructed in the early 1870s, but was in operation less than a year when it was closed due to financial problems.

Although nothing remains, the old hotel was still standing in the 1980s when I would often ride this route. There is a cafe on the right.

At 12.0 miles the road bends left, then right, away from the Mullica River.

The river is named for Eric Mullica, an early Finnish settler who came to New Jersey in 1697. Crowleytown Glass Works was located near Crowley's Landing. Crowleytown and nearby Hermann City are credited by some authorities with manufacturing the first mason jars. There were a number of houses and a factory here in the 1850s and 1860s.[14] With its view of the Mullica, Crowley's Landing is a great place to stop before returning to Batsto. There are picnic tables, grills and sanitary facilities.

**13.9 Entrance to Batsto Village on right. End of tour.**

## Directions: Ride C

**0.0   Exit parking and park entrance road to right on Route 542.**

Road crosses the Mullica River at 0.3 mile.

**0.4   Left on Route 623.**

On the left is a private residence, that incorporates some of the ruins of the Pleasant Mills Paper Mill, which operated from 1880 until about 1920. Lake Nescochague is to the right.

Just south of here is the Forks, the place where the Mullica and Batsto Rivers join. Historically, the river below that point was called the Little Egg Harbor River. During the Revolutionary War, British ships and goods seized by privateering vessels were auctioned here. In one three-month period alone in 1778, privateers brought two dozen ships to various settlements on the Mullica River, including the Forks. Goods seized included linen, silk, shoes, medicines, tobacco, porter, food, salt, nails and frying pans.

**0.8  Right on Jackson Road.**

**1.7  Stop. Straight on Route 542.**

Look for blueberry fields as the road continues through Nesco. At an inn near Nesco, Joe Mulliner, the best-known bandit of the Pine Barrens was captured in 1781. Mulliner was one of many "refugees" or Tory bandits that roamed the Pine Barrens in search of victims. While they tried to hide behind a facade of political motives, most were just crooks. Mulliner's exploits of dancing and drinking were the stuff of legend and he was given a part in the 1855 novel *Kate Aylesford*. After capture, he was transported to Burlington, tried and hanged for treason and robbery.[15]

There is a food market at 3.4 miles, a custard stand at 5.7 miles on the left, another food market at 5.9 miles and a vegetable stand at 6.2 miles.

**6.4  Left on Boyer Avenue.**

Downtown Hammonton is a short distance west of this intersection.

**7.8  Stop. Left on Route 561.**

**11.2  Bear left, still on Route 561, at intersection with Old Egg Harbor Road.**

**12.0  Traffic light. Left on Route 623. Use caution— there is some high speed traffic.**

The Mullica Township recreational facility is on the right at 13.3 miles.

**16.3  Stop. Right on Route 643 south.**

At 17.7 miles the Sweetwater General Store makes a good place for a ride break. The Mullica River can be seen through the houses to the left along portions of this road. Sweetwater Casino Restaurant is located at the end of Seventh Avenue.

**20.2  Left, still on Route 643, at intersection with Route 612.**

**20.5  Left on Route 563 (Weekstown Road).**

This road goes through an area of wetlands as you approach the Mullica River. At 21.9 miles you cross a small bridge.

**22.2  Cross Green Bank Bridge.**

This rustic bridge was once hand-cranked open to allow larger vessels to continue upstream to the Forks. A pizza shop on the right greets you after you get over the bridge.

If you make the first right after crossing the bridge, you will go past a number of nice houses with great river views. In a short distance the road ends at a picnic pavilion and public restrooms. This is part of Green Bank State Forest (administered by Wharton Sate Forest). Green Bank State Forest includes almost 2,000 acres.

**22.3 Left on River Road.**

**22.8 Stop. Left on Route 542.**

Bel Haven Canoe Rentals is across from this intersection. Crowley's Landing lies ahead at 24.3 miles.

**26.1 Entrance to Batsto Village on right. End of tour.**

**An old shed and wagon at Batsto Village.**

# Atsion
## Rides A and B

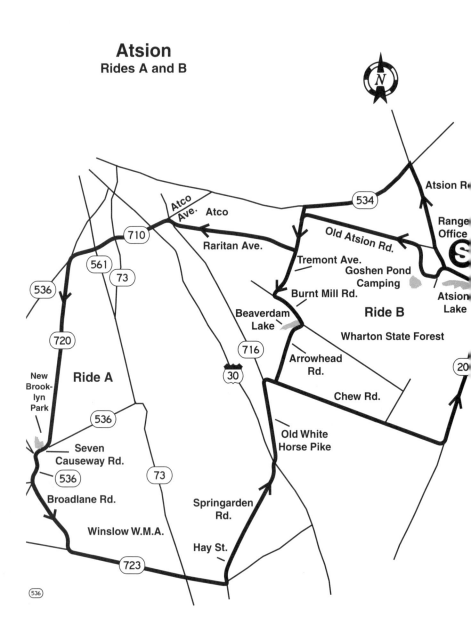

# Atsion

## Start:

Atsion Ranger Headquarters, Wharton State Forest, Burlington County. Route 206 to ranger headquarters on east side of road across from Atsion Lake. Do not park directly in front of ranger building; park on far side of fence in adjacent field. There's more parking at the recreation area adjacent to Atsion Lake. This latter area has public facilities, but is open only from April 1 through October 31. A parking fee is charged at the recreation area.

## Rides:

**Ride A** is 36.9 miles on paved roads with moderate traffic.

**Ride B** is 19.7 miles on paved and dirt/sand road with light to moderate traffic. Route 206 can have heavy, high speed traffic, but there is a wide shoulder.

The name Atsion derives from the Native American name for the area: Atsayunk. As with Batsto, Charles Read was responsible for early development of the area. He built a forge here in the 1760s and subsequent owners built sawmills and a gristmill. However, extensive development didn't take place until the 1820s when Samuel Richards purchased the property. Under Richards a town developed around the various enterprises that employed more than 100 workers. At the time of his death in 1842, Richards owned over 100,000 acres of the surrounding land. During the next few decades, the buildings were used for a paper mill, a cotton mill and agricultural enterprises. Also like Batsto, the area was eventually purchased by Joseph Wharton.

Today only a handful of these buildings remain including the old company store c. 1827 (now the rangers headquarters) and the Richards Mansion, which was built in 1826. This example of Greek Revival architecture is one of the better preserved 19th-century buildings in the Pine Barrens. Guidebooks containing old pictures of this settlement and descriptions of the settlement's history are available at the ranger headquarters. Also available are park and United States Geological Survey quadrangle maps. If you visit between Memorial Day and Labor Day bring your swim suit for a dip in the lake.

Ride A leaves Wharton State Forest and goes through the western edge of the Pine Barrens in Camden and Gloucester counties. Historically, there were thousands of acres of Pine Barrens in these two counties, but much of this land has been altered by development and agriculture. The ride returns through Atlantic County, making it a four-county tour. Ride B has some sections in common with Ride A, but a few sections go off-road through the forest.

## *Directions Ride A:*

**0.0   Exit parking across Route 206 and turn immediately right on Atsion Road (sign for Atco).**

Atsion Lake, which was formed by damming the Mullica River, is on the left. In the 19th century there was an ice-house located on the opposite shore.

Cabins line the road on the left and a canoe rental store sits on the right. At 1.5 miles is a sign for Goshen Pond Camping. This road goes through the state forest and an area of mostly large Pitch Pines.

**4.6   Stop. Left on Route 534 (Jackson Road). Use caution—road is narrow in sections.**

This small crossroads has the name of Dellette. At 6.2 miles the road bends right and then takes you over a small bridge into Camden County. At 7.7 miles Atco Raceway is on the right and you have left the state forest.

**8.0   Left on Tremont Avenue.**

**9.0   Right on Raritan Avenue.**

This road goes through a wooded, partially developed area.

**11.8 Stop. Left on Route 710 (Atco Avenue).**

There are a few convenience stores in downtown Atco.

**12.2 Traffic light. Continue straight at Route 30 intersection, still on Route 710.**

At 12.6 miles the road bends sharply to the right.

**13.1 Traffic light. Continue straight at Route 73 intersection,**

**still on Route 710.**

**13.5 Stop. Continue straight at Route 561 intersection, still on Route 710 (Hayes Mill Road).**

**14.1 Traffic light. Left on Route 536 (Williamstown Road).**

**14.2 Left on Route 720 (New Freedom-New Brooklyn Road).**

At 14.9 miles use caution crossing railroad tracks.

**18.0 Stop. Right on Route 536 (Seven Causeways Road).**

An historic marker describes the Isabella Glassworks which operated from 1832–1856. Thomas Stanger is one of the best known of America's early glassmakers. Items manufactured here are highly prized by collectors.

The 600-acre New Brooklyn Park, Camden County's only Pine Barrens park, lies on the right along this road. The lake was formed by damming the Great Egg Harbor River.

**18.3 Left on Route 536 (Malaga Road).**

At 18.4 miles you cross over the Atlantic City Expressway. At 18.6 miles you cross a small bridge over the Great Egg Harbor River and enter Gloucester County.

**18.8 Left on Broadlane Road.**

At 20.1 miles the road bends sharply to the right.

**20.5 Stop. Left on Route 723 (Winslow Road).**

This road goes through the Winslow Wildlife Management Area. Though the Pinelands National Reserve extends west of this point, this publicly owned land is the last large preserved pinelands parcel in Gloucester County. Like New Brooklyn Park, it straddles the Great Egg Harbor River.

You recross the Great Egg Harbor River and reenter Camden County at 21.2 miles. At 22.5 miles the road goes over the Atlantic City Expressway.

**23.0 Traffic light. Continue straight at intersection with Route 73, still on Route 723.**

Inskip's Sawmill, built in 1762, was located near this intersection. There is an historical marker.

**23.9 Bear sharply to left, still on Route 723.**

**24.0 Left on Hay Street (sign for Ancora Hospital).**

**24.4 Flashing red light. Continue straight across intersection**

**with South Egg Harbor Road, now on Springarden Road.**

Use caution crossing railroad tracks at 24.7 miles.

Ancora Hospital is a state psychiatric facility. The road bends sharply left at 26.5 miles.

**26.7 Traffic light. Continue straight across Route 30, now on Route 716 (Old White Horse Pike). Road bends immediately left.**

The road goes through a swampy area that is part of the state forest.

**27.6 Use caution on the narrow bridge over the railroad.**

**28.4 Right on Route 536 (Chew Road).**

This small town, Waterford Works, is named after a glass factory that operated here from the 1820s through the 1890s.

The road enters Wharton State Forest at 29.8 miles, heavily forested on both sides. You enter Atlantic County at 33.0 miles.

**33.8 Stop. Left on Route 206 north. There can be heavy traffic. Use wide shoulder.**

At 34.1 miles there is a large blueberry operation and a large wetlands area at 35.1 miles. There is a restaurant at 35.5 miles. You enter Burlington County at 36.0 miles.

**36.7 Atsion Recreation Area and Atsion Lake on the left.**

**36.9 Ranger Headquarters parking on right. End of tour.**

## Direction: Ride B.

**0.0 Exit parking across Route 206 and turn immediately right on Atsion Road (sign for Atco).**

**1.5 Left at sign for Goshen Pond Camping (unnamed dirt road).**

**1.9 Right at campsite sign.**

Goshen Pond and campsite are at 2.2 miles. All campers must register at the ranger's office.

**2.5 Right on unnamed dirt road. There is a low spot here adjacent to the pond.**

**3.4 Left on Old Atsion Road (unmarked/dirt).**

**4.1** **Continue straight at unnamed intersection, still on Old Atsion Road. The road narrows at this point and becomes sandier.**

**4.6** **Use caution crossing bridge over the Mullica River. This is the border between Burlington and Camden counties.**

**5.2** **Continue straight at unnamed intersection, still on Old Atsion Road.**

There is a shooting range on the left, and the road is paved at Columbia Avenue.

**7.3** **Stop. Left on Tremont Avenue.**

**8.3** **Continue straight through intersection with Raritan Avenue, still on Tremont Avenue.**

**8.6** **Continue straight, as road becomes dirt at Martha Road intersection.**

Reenter Wharton State Forest.

**8.9** **Cross small bridge over Hays Mill Creek.**

**9.2** **Left on Burnt Mill Road (unmarked).**

The road goes through a swampy area and can have large water holes. Beaverdam Lake (private) is on the right at 9.6 miles.

**10.1** **Use caution at stream crossing.**

**10.2** **Right on unnamed road.**

There are a few houses on the right.

**Ride Option**: To continue through the forest keep straight on Burnt Mill Road for 3.4 miles. At railroad tracks turn right and parallel the railroad tracks until you reach Route 536.

**10.4** **Bear left on Arrowhead (Church) Road (paved).**

The New Jersey Public Broadcasting facility is on the right.

**11.5** **Stop. Left on Route 536 (Chew Road).**

**16.6** **Stop. Left on Route 206. Use caution, there can be heavy traffic. Use wide shoulder.**

**19.7** **Ranger headquarters parking on right. End of tour.**

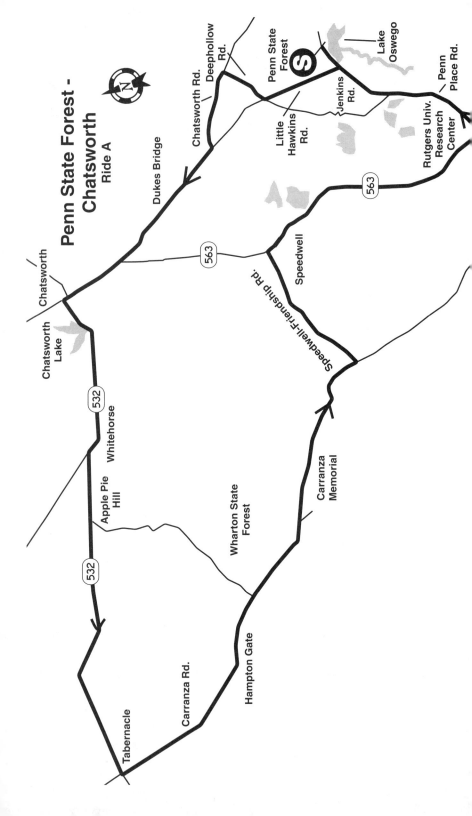

# Penn State Forest - Chatsworth
## Ride A

# Penn State Forest - Chatsworth

## Start:

Lake Oswego, Penn State Forest, Burlington County. Route 72 to Route 563 or Route 532 to Chatsworth. Continue south on Route 563 for nine miles. Left on Penn Place Road which joins Jenkins Road (unmarked). Continue past Rutgers Research Center to parking at Lake Oswego.

## Rides:

**Ride A** is 37.4 miles on paved and dirt/sand roads with light to moderate traffic.

**Ride B** is 17.7 miles on dirt/sand roads and narrow sand trails (small section is paved) with almost no traffic.

The cranberry *(Vaccinium macrocarpon)*, along with the blueberry *(Vaccinium corymbosum)*, are the two agricultural products most associated with the Pine Barrens. Both originally grew wild and were introduced to early settlers by Native Americans. The cranberry was picked for food and medicine and crushed to make dye by Native-Americans who called the plant Pakim. It is said early settlers named it the crane-berry because the curving flower heads resembled the head of the bird. By 1840, following the lead of Cape Cod growers, wild plants were transplanted and domestic cranberry harvesting began in the Pine Barrens.

Cranberry growing and harvesting is a fascinating process. The plants are grown in low fields (commonly called bogs) surrounded by dikes and connected by sluiceways and ditches. When the fruit ripens in fall, the fields are flooded and the fruit beaten from vines by machines pushed through the water. The berries float to the surface and are gathered by booms toward conveyors that lift the fruit into trucks on the edge of the bogs.

Today, annual Pine Barrens' cranberry production totals more than 50 million pounds, with an estimated worth of more than $20 million. Most of the crop goes to the nearby Ocean Spray receiving warehouse and from there is shipped to factories in Bordentown, N.J. and Massachusetts, where it is processed into juice and sauce. A small portion of the crop is picked and bagged as fresh fruit.

Ride A goes through one of the most productive cranberry areas in the pines. It connects Chatsworth, the best-known Pine Barrens town with some other historic sites including the Carranza Memorial and Speedwell. Fall is a great time for this ride when harvesting can be observed first hand. Chatsworth hosts the Cranberry Festival every October.

Ride B goes through a large portion of the pygmy pine forest, which is an internationally famous ecological area of the pines. The starting point, Lake Oswego, is part of Penn State Forest and is administered by nearby Bass River State Forest. Call (609) 296-1114 for further information.

## *Directions: Ride A*

**0.0  Exit parking to left on Jenkins Road.**

Cross bridge over Lake Oswego. Lake Oswego was formed by damming the Oswego River. This river is a tributary of the Wading River which flows south into the Mullica.

**0.1  Right on Little Hawkins Road (unmarked/first dirt road after crossing bridge).**

**1.5  Right on Deephollow Road (unmarked/first crossroads).**

At 1.9 miles this road enters a swampy area.

**2.3  Left on Chatsworth Road (unmarked).**

This road is heavily rutted in areas. At 4.0 miles there is a small bridge and at 4.3 miles the road becomes paved.

**5.7  Continue straight at intersection to right and cross two small bridges at Dukes Bridge.**

**6.7  Stop. Continue straight, now on Route 563.**

Just south of this intersection is the Ocean Spray Cranberry warehouse.

At 7.4 miles you enter Chatsworth. Across from the intersection with Route 532 is the former location of Buzby's General Store. It was originally built in 1865 and was run by the Buzby family for 80 years.

On the right, as you continue through town and cross the abandoned railway, is the White Horse Inn (formerly Shamong Hotel). This early 20th-century structure, now slated for renovation, was part of the Chatsworth Country Club (see next mileage description).

**7.6  Left on Route 532.**

Chatsworth Lake appears on the right a short distance after you turn. Prince Ruspoli, an Italian diplomat, built a large vacation villa on the shores of the lake in the 1890s. Many wealthy socialites, including the Astors, Morgans and Vanderbilts visited the prince. A large guest mansion, the Chatsworth Country Club, was built next to the villa. Other buildings were constructed for visitors, who came by train from New York and Philadelphia. The club's popularity faded and only the White Horse Inn still remains.

The White Horse Tavern historical marker is at 11.1 miles. The tavern operated from the 1790s through the first half of the 19th century. This was also the site of Paisley or Magic City. In the 1880s, real estate developers tried to build a 1400-acre city in the pines. The city was to have thousands of inhabitants and an accompanying infrastructure. Only a few buildings were ever constructed.[16]

To the south of this road is Apple Pie Hill at 205 feet, the highest point in the Pine Barrens. Continue past Moores Meadow Road intersection at 12.7 miles.

**14.5  Bear right at Goose Pond, still on Route 532.**

**15.5  Bear left, still on Route 532 at intersection with New Road.**

As you enter Tabernacle, the pines give way to an area of produce farms. Nixon's General Store is a good place to stop for a ride break.

**17.3  Four-way stop. Left on Carranza Road.**

There is a large produce market at this intersection.

As you continue along this road the pavement gets progressively rougher. At 20.9 miles you enter Wharton State Forest. At 21.1 miles you cross a narrow bridge over the Batsto River. Located a short distance from here was Hampton Furnace. This furnace produced tools, wagon axles and iron bar. It probably ceased production in 1829. At 22.2 miles is a juvenile correction facility and at 22.4 miles you cross a small bridge over Skit Branch.

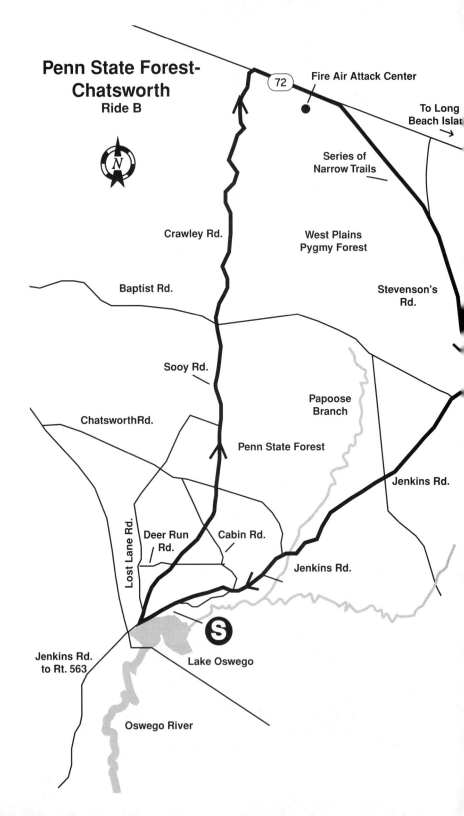

# Penn State Forest-
# Chatsworth
## Ride B

Fire Air Attack Center

72

To Long
Beach Island

Series of
Narrow Trails

Crawley Rd.

West Plains
Pygmy Forest

Baptist Rd.

Stevenson's
Rd.

Sooy Rd.

Papoose
Branch

ChatsworthRd.

Penn State Forest

Jenkins Rd.

Lost Lane Rd.

Deer Run
Rd.

Cabin Rd.

Jenkins Rd.

Jenkins Rd.
to Rt. 563

Lake Oswego

Oswego River

## 23.9 Carranza Memorial.

On July 13, 1928 (yes, a Friday) Emilio Carranza's airplane crashed in a thunderstorm near this small clearing. Carranza was attempting to fly non-stop from New York to Mexico City as a goodwill gesture from the Mexican to the American people. Charles Lindbergh had made a similiar flight in 1927. Carranza's body was discovered by local residents a few days after the crash and returned by rail to Mexican City where he was buried with full military honors.[17]

Each year, American Legion Post No. 11 from Mount Holly holds a ceremony at the memorial honoring the airman. Attendees often include members of the Mexican Consulates from Washington and New York and relatives of Carranza.

The Batona Trail crosses the road at this point.

At 25.2 miles the road turns completely to dirt. You continue over a few small bridges and enter a lowland area of small bogs and wetlands. This is a good place to look for orchids, including Moccasin-flower (*Cypripedium acaule*).

## 27.2 Left on Speedwell-Friendship Road. Turn immediately after crossing small bridge over Shane Branch.

Along this road was the Eagle Tavern which operated in the first half of the 19th century. It was popular with travelers and nearby mill workers. The road becomes paved at 28.8 miles.

## 29.7 Stop. Right on Route 563.

Speedwell was the location of an 18th- and 19th-century sawmill and furnace. Daniel Randolph built a sawmill here around 1770 and sold it to his brother Benjamin. Benjamin built an iron furnace which, under a subsequent owner, operated until the 1840s. It is said that Benjamin, who was also a furniture maker, made the desk upon which Thomas Jefferson wrote the Declaration of Independence.

After turning, you cross a bridge over the West Branch of the Wading River, a popular launching spot for canoe trips.

As you continue south along Route 563 there are large cranberry bogs on both sides of the road. Each acre planted in cranberries requires ten additional acres of surrounding wetlands for production.

There is a canoe rental outfitter to the left at 3.1 miles.

**34.2 Left on Penn Place Road (unmarked).**

The Rutgers University Blueberry and Cranberry Research Center is located at 35.5 miles.

At 37.3 miles you cross a small bridge.

**37.4 Lake Oswego parking. End of tour.**

## Directions: Ride B

**0.0 Exit parking to right. Pavement immediately turns to dirt.**

As you follow these directions, be aware that there are no street signs and very few landmarks. If you pay attention to mileage and crossroads, you should find the directions easy to follow. The route starts north through Penn State Forest.

**0.1 Left on Sooy Road (unmarked). This is the first road to the left.**

**0.2 Bear right, still on Sooy Road (unmarked).**

**0.9 Continue straight, still on Sooy Road, at intersection with Deer Run Road (unmarked).**

**1.4 Continue straight, still on Sooy Road, at intersection with Cabin Road.**

A few sections of this road are paved.

**2.0 Continue straight, still on Sooy Road, at intersection with Chatsworth Road.**

Sections of the road are gravelly, others hard packed dirt.

**2.7 Continue straight, now on Crawley Road, at intersection with Lane Road.**

The route leaves Penn State Forest and goes up a slight hill into the West Plains Pygmy Forest. The surface is very thick sugar sand for most of the ride through the pygmy forest.

There are about 20 square miles of dwarf or pygmy forest in the Pine Barrens. The dominant trees are the Pitch Pine *(Pinus rigida)* and Black-jack Oak *(Quercus maralandica)*. Neither usually exceeds ten feet in height in the plains, even though they grow to 70 and 40 feet respectively elsewhere. Understory species include Bearberry *(Arctostaphylos uva-ursi)*, trailing Arbutus *(Epigaea repens)* and Teaberry *(Gaultheria procumbens)*.

Riding through this forest and standing on my pedals, I can see over the top of the forest in some places and I am only 5'8". Frequent fires, poor soil quality and wind have all been suggested as causes of the unique stunted tree growth.

**5.8**   **Bear sharp to left, still on Crawley Road (unmarked).**

**6.8**   **Bear sharply to left around gate, still on Crawley Road.**

Sugar sand gives way to gravel. Keep to left around fenced area.

**7.3**   **Stop. Right on Route 72. (You can ride on sand/dirt trail which parallels Route 72).**

You go up a hill with views of the pygmy forest from both sides of the road.

**8.4**   **Right on Stevenson Road (unmarked). It is the first dirt road after the fire service sign. Keep straight through series of intersections with trails.**

**8.8**   **Continue straight at intersection with trail on right.**

**9.2**   **Continue straight as road narrows to trail width.**

**10.2**   **Right on Stevenson's Road (unmarked). This is a wide, mostly dirt road.**

**12.5**   **Road bends to right, now on Jenkins Road (unmarked).**

There is a bog area on the left.

**15.4**   **Bear to right, still on Jenkins Road.**

This is a lowland area of meadows and bogs. At 15.6 miles you cross a small bridge over the Papoose Branch of the Oswego River.

The road is roughly paved in sections. Continue through series of intersections, staying on wider road.

**17.7**   **Lake Oswego parking. End of tour.**

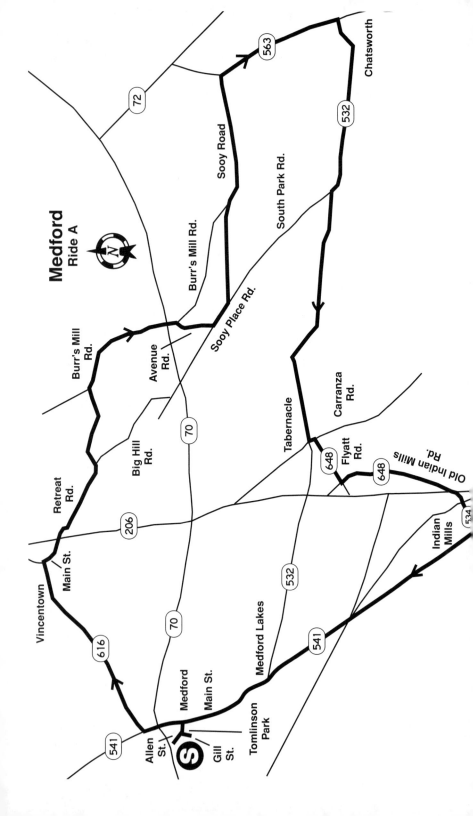

# Medford

## Start:

Tomlinson Park, Medford, Burlington County. Route 70 to Main Street. South on Main Street to Allen Street. Right on Allen Street to Gill Street. Left on Gill Street to parking adjacent to park.

## Rides:

**Ride A** is 46.2 miles on paved roads with light to heavy traffic.

**Ride B** is 21.8 miles on paved roads with moderate to heavy traffic.

The first inhabitants of New Jersey were the Lenni-Lenape. Sometimes translated as meaning "original people," the Lenni-Lenape were a loose confederation of tribes organized into three nations: the Minsi in the north, the Unami in the central and the Unalchtigo in the south. Part of the larger Algonquin nation, they were generally viewed, even scorned, by other Algonquins as a peaceful confederation. Most of their villages were located in the western part of the state and they used a system of trails to travel to the coast for seasonal hunting, fishing and the gathering of shells to make wampum.

When Europeans arrived in the early 1600s, these native peoples were at peace and, although maybe not by the newcomers' standards, prosperous. This didn't last long. First the Dutch, then the English brought guns, disease and liquor. Never numerous to begin with (the estimated population in 1600 was a few thousand) there were probably fewer than 500 Lenni-Lenape by 1700. Most of their land had been sold. Many of these treaties were signed by chiefs who were unfamiliar with the European concept of land ownership.

In 1758 the New Jersey legislature "gave" the remaining few hundred Indians 3,285 acres in Burlington County. This tract became known as the Brotherton Indian Reservation. The reservation lasted until 1801 when the few remaining Indians left for New York and the land was sold back to the state. Although the reservation is long gone, it is an interesting historical site because it was the first Native-American reservation anywhere.

Ride A goes by this site, which is now called Indian Mills. It also goes by a number of other historical sites in the Pine Barrens and surrounding countryside, including two sites associated with the "Doctor of the Pines" (see below). Ride B is a shorter ride through a more developed area west of Medford. Be aware that there can be heavy traffic on parts of both of these rides.

## Directions: Ride A

**0.0  Exit park on Gill Street to Allen Street.**

**0.1  Stop. Right on Allen Street.**

**0.3  Stop. Left on Main Street.**

Downtown Medford has some restaurants and stores. Stock up before you start the ride.

Medford was originally called Bella Bridge and later Upper Evesham. It acquired its current name in 1828.

**0.5  Traffic light. Continue straight at intersection with Union, still on Main Street.**

**0.8  Traffic light. Continue straight at intersection with Route 70, now on Route 541 north.**

**1.6  Traffic light. Right on Route 616 (Church Road).**

The house on the left was the home and office of James Still. Known as the "Doctor of the Pines," Still was a self-taught herbalist who treated the people of the area until his death in 1885. He was the son of slaves who bought their freedom and moved to the area from Maryland. When he was in his twenties, Still started experimenting with local plants and roots and developed a number of cures. Although he was initially met with a lot of skepticism, especially from the white medical community, his cures proved effective. He became well known throughout the area and he made a comfortable living by selling his remedies to Philadelphia druggists. The house is not open to the public.[18]

**2.1  Bear left, still on Route 616 (Church Road).**

At 2.7 miles is Kirby's Mill. The original mill dated from 1778.

**3.2   Continue straight at intersection with Eayrestown Road, still on Route 616.**

At 3.7 miles you cross a small bridge.

**4.4   Flashing yellow light. Continue straight at intersection with Eayrestown Road, still on Route 616.**

**6.0   Stop. Right on Main Street.**

There is a pizza shop, a cafe and some antique stores in downtown Vincentown. Vincentown is named after Vincent Leeds, an early settler.

**6.6   Traffic light. Continue straight at intersection with Route 206, now on Retreat Road.**

At 6.9 you cross a small narrow bridge.

**7.9   Four-way stop. Continue straight at intersection with Ridge Road, still on Retreat Road.**

**8.5   Bear left, at intersection with Big Hill Road, still on Retreat Road.**

In the 19th century there was a small settlement here called Retreat. Located nearby were a cotton factory, two iron forges, a blacksmith shop and a sawmill. There was also a large boardinghouse which was frequented by Lottie Cushman, one of the most accomplished actresses of the mid-19th century.

The land on which some of these buildings stood is slated for development. Under pinelands regulations the land must first be excavated by archaeologists. This project is currently underway and could provide valuable information about Pine Barrens life.

As you continue down this road you will cross some more small bridges and go past Thompson's U-Pick blueberry farm at 9.4 miles. Continue over a narrow bridge at 9.9 miles and a cranberry bog at 10.0. miles.

**10.3 Right on Burr's Mill Road (rough in sections).**

**12.8 Stop. Continue straight at intersection with Route 70, still on Burr's Mill Road (use caution).**

At 13.0 miles cross small bridge over Burr's Mill Creek.

**13.0 Bear right on Avenue Road (unmarked).**

**13.2 Bear left, still on Avenue Road.**

Continue through small housing development.

**13.9 Stop. Left on Sooy Place Road.**

**14.4 Bear left, at intersection with South Park Road, still on Sooy Place Road.**

This road goes through a long stretch of undisturbed Pine Barrens.

**16.5 Bear right, still on Sooy Place Road.**

At 17.3 miles there is a lake to the right.

**20.1 Stop. Right on Route 563.**

The Hedger House Tavern is at 20.4 miles on the right.

**23.1 Right on Route 532. Stay on Route 532 as it twists through the Pine Barrens.**

(For more specific instructions and descriptions of Chatsworth and various sites between here and Tabernacle, refer to the Penn State Forest-Chatsworth chapter.)

At 32.8 miles Nixon's General Store is a good place for a ride break.

**32.9 Stop. Left on Route 648 (Carranza Road).**

**33.0 Right on Route 648, now called Flyatt Road.**

In season, the magnificent displays of local produce will make you want to stop at Conte Farms market.

**34.1 Left on Route 648 South, now called Old Indian Mills Road.**

At 35.0 miles is the former location of the Union School, which was built in 1860.

**35.5 Bear to right at intersection with Tuckerton Road, still on Route 648.**

**36.8 Stop. Continue straight across intersection with Route 206, now on Route 534 (Willow Grove Road). Use caution crossing Route 206.**

There is a restaurant at this intersection.

This was the center of the Brotherton Indian Reservation. The reservation's sawmills, church and various other buildings were located along this road. Historical markers describe some of these buildings and their location. For more information on local and regional Native American history and culture visit the Rankokus Reservation which is located in nearby Rancocas. Call (609) 261-4747 for more information and directions.

**37.2 Stop. Continue straight at intersection with Route 620**

**(Medford-Indian Mills Road) and Burnt House Road, still on Willow Grove Road.**

A large historical marker at this location describes the reservation.

**37.9 Stop. Right on Route 541 (Stokes Road).**

An historical marker at 38.3 miles describes the Shamong Trail, which was one of the main Native-American trails in the state.

There is a small lake on the left at 38.5 miles.

**38.9 Four-way stop. Continue straight at intersection with Oakshade Road, still on route 541.**

At 39.7 miles there is an historical marker noting the location of James Still's childhood home. In Still's autobiography, which was published in 1877, he wrote about the poverty endured by his family.

**41.0 Continue straight at intersection with Route 620, still on Route 541. Caution, there can be heavy traffic the rest of the ride.**

There are a number of private lakes as you continue through aptly named Medford Lakes.

**43.5 Traffic light. Continue straight at intersection with Route 532 (Tabernacle Road).**

On the right is the Settlers Inn, one of largest two- story log buildings in America.

There are a number of stores and restaurants along this stretch of road.

**44.2 Traffic light. Bear left at intersection with Dixontown Road, still on Route 541.**

**44.4 Traffic light. Continue straight at intersection with Jackson Road, still on Route 541.**

You reenter Medford after passing by a farm on the right.

**45.9 Left on Allen Street.**

**46.1 Left on Gill Street.**

**46.2 Tomlinson Park parking on left. End of tour.**

# Medford Lakes
## Ride B

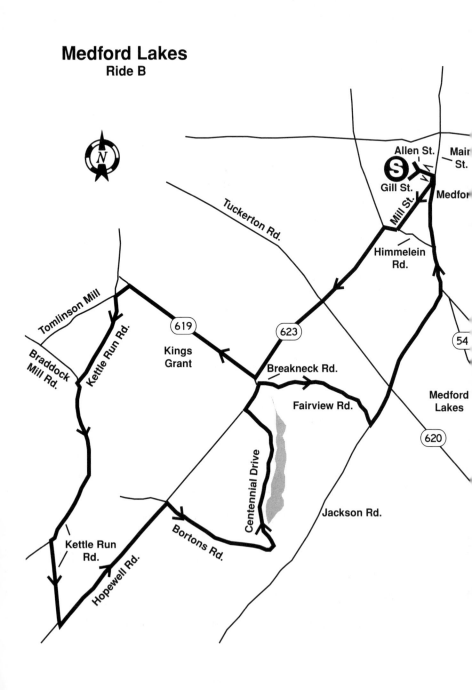

Allen St.

Main St.

Gill St.

Medfor

Mill St.

Himmelein Rd.

Tuckerton Rd.

Tomlinson Mill

Kettle Run Rd.

619

623

Breakneck Rd.

Kings Grant

54

Fairview Rd.

Braddock Mill Rd.

Medford Lakes

620

Centennial Drive

Kettle Run Rd.

Bortons Rd.

Jackson Rd.

Hopewell Rd.

# Directions: Ride B

**0.0  Exit park on Gill Street to Allen Street.**

**O.1  Stop. Right on Allen Street.**

**0.3  Stop. Right on Main Street.**

**0.4  Right on Mill Street.**
Cross small bridge at 0.7 mile.

**1.1  Stop. Right on Route 623 (Himmelein Road).**

**1.3  Traffic light. Left on Route 623 (Taunton Boulevard). Use caution, moderate to heavy traffic for the next five miles.**
At 1.6 miles Oliphant's Lake is visible through the houses to the left.

**2.4  Traffic light. Continue straight at intersection with Tuckerton Road, still on Route 623.**
There are stores at this intersection.
This residential area is called Taunton Forge, after the forge and furnace that operated here from the 1760s to about 1835. It was owned by Charles Read, who also started Batsto and Atsion.

**3.8  Traffic light. Right on Route 619 (Tomlinson Mill Road).**

**4.9  Traffic light. Continue straight at Kings Grant entrance, still on Route 619.**
Kings Grant is one of the largest housing projects to be approved in the pinelands since restrictions were implemented almost 20 years ago.
Use caution crossing the small bridge at 5.3 miles.

**5.9  Traffic light. Left on Tomlinson Mill Road.**
Jennings Lake is on the right. Take care in crossing metal grated bridge.

**6.2  Bear left on Kettle Run Road.**
This road enters an area of mostly undisturbed Pine Barrens.

**7.4  Bear left at Braddock Mill Rd. intersection, still on Kettle Run Road.**
The road bends through a lowland area that was formerly cranberry bogs. It then bends through an upland area of mostly Pitch Pines.

**9.7 Left on Kettle Run Road (Sycamore Avenue is straight).**

A housing development appears along this road.

**10.7 Stop. Left on Hopewell Road.**

There is a lake to the right at this intersection.

**12.6 Right on Bortons Road. Enter Preserve at Little Mill housing development.**

**14.2 Left on Centennial Drive.**

Continue through the housing development. Centennial Lake is visible through the houses to the right. At 15.5 you can turn right and go over Dam Road to get a better view of the lake. Cross a small bridge at 16.0 miles.

**16.1 Stop. Right on Hopewell Road.**

**16.5 Stop. Right on Breakneck Road.**

Centennial Lake bathing beach is to the right.

**16.7 Bear left, still on Breakneck Road.**

**16.8 Continue straight (a little right) on Fairview Road.**

**18.2 Stop. Left on Jackson Road. Use caution, there can be heavy traffic the rest of the ride.**

**18.7 Traffic light. Continue straight at intersection with Tuckerton Road, still on Jackson Road.**

**20.1 Traffic light. Left on Route 541 (Stokes Road).**

**21.5 Left on Allen Street.**

**21.7 Left on Gill Street.**

**21.8 Tomlinson Park parking on left. End of tour.**

A lush growth of bracken ferns fills the woods after a fire.

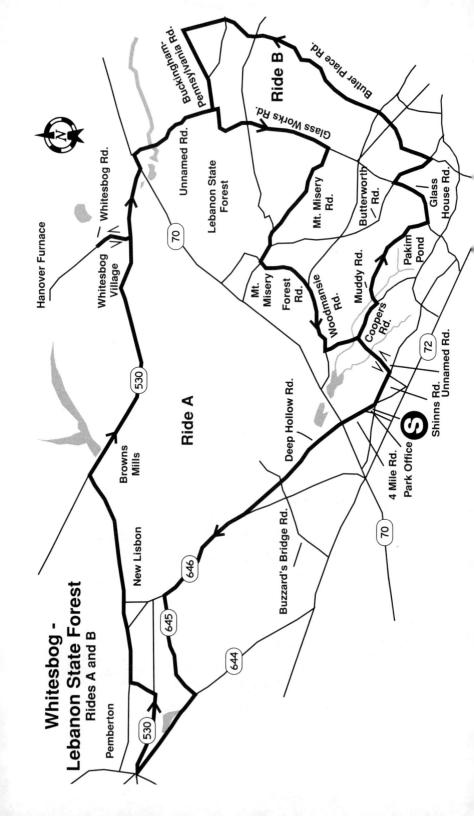

# Whitesbog - Lebanon State Forest

## Start:

Lebanon State Forest Park Office, Lebanon State Forest, Burlington County. Route 70 to Route 72 south. Turn left at sign for park office. Turn right on Shinns Road. Parking is located on left adjacent to office. (Additional parking is available adjacent to Pakim Pond).

## Rides:

**Ride A** is 32.6 miles on paved and dirt/sand roads with light to heavy traffic.

**Ride B** is 22.3 miles on paved and dirt/sand roads with light traffic.

Lebanon State Forest contains over 31,000 acres of upland forest and lowland cedar swamps. It gets its name from the Lebanon Glassworks which operated here between 1851 and 1867. Other area enterprises included clay mining and tile manufacturing at Pasadena and sawmills at Mount Misery and Buckingham. One of the largest Pine Barrens iron furnaces operated at Hanover in the early 19th century. The forest has reclaimed most of these sites and there is very little evidence that they ever existed. However, many buildings remain in Whitesbog Village, a center for cranberry and blueberry production in the 19th and early 20th century.

In 1910 Elizabeth White invited botanist Frederick Colville to her family's home to test his theories about blueberry hybridization. Local residents were paid to scour the pines and identify those wild Highbush Blueberry *(Vaccinium corymbosum)* plants that produced the largest berries. These bushes were gathered from the surrounding area and the best were transplanted. Hybrids were made, and today most cultivated blueberries in North America come from these plants. Elizabeth White also pioneered the use of cellophane packing on cartons to protect the berries.

Today efforts to restore Whitesbog Village are under way. The Whitesbog Preservation Trust also conducts historical and ecological tours. Ride A leaves the state forest going through Browns Mills before returning past Whitesbog Village and continuing through the heart of the state forest to Mount Misery. Ride B goes through the state forest to the former location of Buckingham, before returning along the same route as Ride A. Forest maps are available at the park office. You can also purchase U.S.G.S quadrangle maps for serious exploration of the area. Bring a swimsuit, and cool off with a swim in Pakim Pond after your ride.

## *Directions: Ride A*

**0.0  Exit parking left on 4 Mile Road.**

**0.7  Stop. Continue straight at intersection with Route 70, now on Deep Hollow Road. Use caution.**

This road continues through the state forest. The Presidential Lakes housing development is to the right.

The road becomes increasingly rough and turns to gravel at 1.4 miles.

**2.2  Continue straight at intersection with Buzzard's Bridge Road (unmarked), still on Deep Hollow Road.**

Deep Hollow Road narrows at this point and becomes sandy.

**3.0  Stop. Right on Route 646 (New Lisbon Road). Paved.**

**5.1  Left on Route 645 (New Lisbon-Magnolia Road).**

This road goes through a wetlands area. Cross small bridge at 5.9 miles.

**7.0  Stop. Right on Route 644 (Magnolia Road).**

The Pemberton Lake Wildlife Management Area is on the right. Its lake is a nice place for a ride break, and a deli can be found at 8.3 miles.

**8.7  Traffic light. Right on Route 530 (Pemberton Parkway).**

The lake and wetlands area is now on your right as you leave Pemberton. The road bends left at 10.0 miles.

**10.7  Right on Route 530 (Pemberton-Browns Mills Road).**

Fort Dix Military Reservation is on the left along part of this road. Also on this road are Burlington County College, a county work release facility and a sports complex.

There is more traffic as you enter Browns Mills.

**14.4 Traffic light. Right on Route 530 (Lakehurst Road). Use caution, there can be heavy traffic as you ride through Browns Mills. Continue straight through two more traffic lights.**

Stores and fast food restaurants abound in town. The lake was formed by damming Rancocas Creek. This entire region of the Pine Barrens is part of the Rancocas Creek Watershed, the only Pine Barrens watershed that drains westward.

**16.8 Traffic light. Continue straight at intersection with Ridge Road, still on Route 530.**

**17.9 Bear right, still on Route 530.**

**18.9 Left on Whitesbog Road (sign for Whitesbog Village). Pavement is rough and narrow in sections.**

**19.5 Whitesbog Village (Return to Route 530).**

Check out the bulletin board in the center of the village. It has informational brochures and maps detailing the location and function of the various buildings.

Hanover Furnace and Forge was located a short distance north of here. (It is now within the boundaries of Fort Dix.) A village of almost 1,000 residents surrounded the operation. The furnace and forge produced a number of items, including cannon balls for the War of 1812.

**20.1 Stop. Left on Route 530.**

There are large cranberry bogs on both sides of this road. The first of them in this area were formed in 1857.

**21.3 Stop. Left (almost straight) on Route 70. Use caution.**

**21.6 Right on unnamed dirt Road (BBB sign on tree).**

At 21.9 miles you cross a small bridge. A spectacular cedar swamp envelops both sides of this road. Reportedly the largest Atlantic White Cedar *(Chamaecyparis thyoides)* in New Jersey is located here. Cedar swamps can contain as many as 4,000 trees per acre.

Cedar swamps are a good place to look for insectivorous plants. The Pitcher-plant *(Sarraceniaceae purpurea)* has a long (up to 2 feet) stalk topped by a large crimson flower that blooms in late May to early June. The plant has pitcher-shaped leaves, which trap insects.

**23.3 Cross intersection and bear right after going under power lines.**

**23.7 Bear left, now on Glass Works Road (unmarked).**

Cross small bridge over the North Branch of Mount Misery Brook at 24.0 miles. An Atlantic White Cedar research project growth area is at 24.5 miles.

As you continue through the woods a common plant to look for in the open areas near the road is Heath-like Hudsonia *(Hudsonia ericoides)*. This very low shrub blooms with tiny yellow flowers in May.

**25.7 Right on Mount Misery Road (unmarked/paved).**

Stay on the paved road as it continues through the forest and climbs slightly to Mount Misery. Cross small bridge over the South Branch of Mount Misery Brook at 27.6 miles.

**28.1 Left on Forest Road (unmarked/dirt). This is the road just before the conference center.**

It is uncertain how Mount Misery got its harsh name. As early as the 1730s there was a sawmill here and in the late 1800s, a small settlement. If the leaves are off the trees to the right (before you turn) there is indeed a view from this 100-foot-high "mountain."

**29.1 Right on Woodmansie Road (unmarked/"T" intersection.)**

Lake on left at 29.9 miles.

**30.4 Left on Coopers Road (unmarked/dirt).**

Immediately cross small bridge over McDonalds Branch and second bridge over Coopers Branch.

**31.0 Right on unnamed road (dirt/sand).**

Cross small bridge over Shinns Branch at 31.3 miles. There is another spectacular cedar swamp along this road.

**31.9 Stop. Right on Shinns Road (unmarked/paved).**

**32.6 Forest ranger's office parking on right. End of tour.**

# Directions: Ride B

**0.0**  **Exit parking to left on Shinn Road.**

**0.7**  **Left on unnamed dirt road.**

At 1.3 miles cross bridge over Shinns Branch and go through cedar swamp.

**1.6**  **Right on Coopers Road (unmarked/dirt).**

**2.3**  **Left on Muddy Road (unmarked dirt/sand).**

If you continue straight, you will reach the camping area and Pakim Pond in about one mile.
This road initially goes through a wetlands area. Look for Mountain-laurel (Kalmia latifolia) in this area. Its large white flowers brighten the woods in late spring.

**2.5**  **Bear sharp right, still on Muddy Road.**

The road narrows at 3.7 miles.

**4.4**  **Left on Glass House Road (unmarked/very rough pavement). This is a "T" intersection that is gated to the right.**

**5.4**  **Right on Butterworth Road (unmarked/dirt). This is another "T" intersection.**

**6.2**  **Left on Butler Place Road (unmarked/dirt). Stay on main dirt road through intersections with narrower roads and trails.**

**8.1**  **Continue straight at intersection with Mount Misery Road (unmarked/paved), still on Butler Place Road.**

Stay on main road through intersections with narrower roads. Cross small bridge at 10.5 miles and continue through wetlands formed by North Branch of Mount Misery Brook.

**11.6** **Stop. Left on Buckingham-Pennsylvania Road (unmarked).**

Buckingham was located near this intersection. There were a few houses and a sawmill that operated from 1880–1895. The rail line ran from Camden to Toms River.

**13.0** **Left on unnamed road (dirt/sand). This road immediately bears right.**

At this point, follow directions for Ride A from 23.3 miles until finish.

**22.3** **Forest ranger's office parking on right. End of tour.**

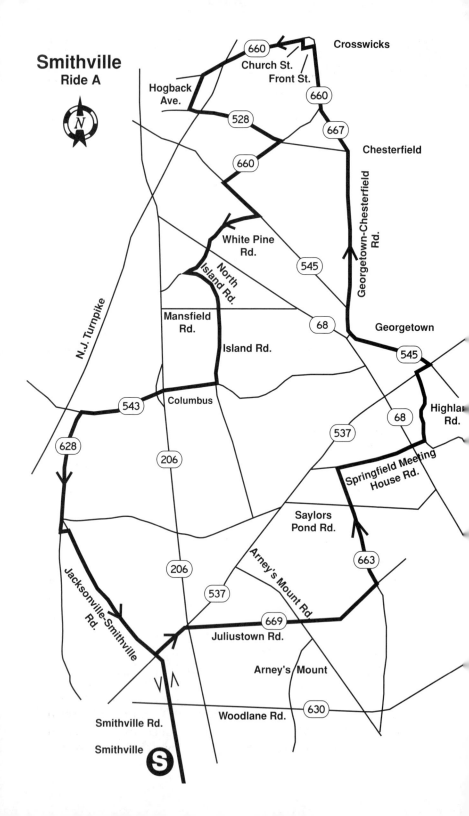

# Smithville

## Start:

Smithville County Park, Burlington County. Route 38 to Smithville Road. Smithville County Park is 0.9 mile from this intersection. Turn left on Mead Road to parking.

## Rides:

**Ride A** is 37.9 miles on paved roads (two short sections of gravel/dirt) with light to heavy traffic.

**Ride B** is 17.3 miles on paved roads with light to moderate traffic.

In the 1870s, before the development of reliable chain drive, riding a bicycle could be a hazardous hobby. Perched precariously on top of a high wheeler, a cyclist could have his center of gravity five and a half feet off the ground and well forward. When the solid tire on the large front wheel would hit a rock or hole the rider would be hurtled toward the ground. And remember, the bike helmet was still a hundred years away. Ouch! Realizing that a dead or injured cyclist would hardly be a future customer, bike manufacturers started to work on the problem.

The Star bicycle was manufactured here by Hezekiah Smith in the 1880s. It had a 20-inch front wheel and a 39-inch rear wheel. The rider sat over the rear wheel powering the bike by a treadle mechanism, rather than having the pedal and crank arms attached directly to the wheel. After mounting the bike during a running start, the cyclist was in a much more stable position than a rider on a high wheeler. The bike became very popular before the widespread introduction of the chain driven "safety" bicycle, the forerunner of today's bicycles. The few remaining Star bicycles are highly sought after by collectors.[19]

Hezekiah Smith moved here in the 1860s from Lowell, Massachusetts, and developed a large industrial complex. Besides manufacturing the Star bicycle, Smith produced woodworking machinery and other mechanical items. In the 1890s, workers rode on a unique bicycle railway to the factory from nearby Mount Holly. Call (609) 265-5068 for more information about the park and annual events.

Ride A starts out along the edge of the Pine Barrens before continuing through the farmland and small towns of northern Burlington County. The ride goes by three historic Friends' Meeting Houses. Ride B is a shorter route through Vincentown and Birmingham. Both rides go over Arney's Mount, which is the high point in the area.

## Directions: Ride A

**0.0   Exit parking to left on Smithville Road.**

**0.3   Stop. Continue straight at intersection with Powell Road, still on Smithville Road.**

Continue through area of housing developments.

**1.1   Traffic light. Continue straight at intersection with Woodlane Road, still on Smithville Road.**

**2.0   Traffic light. Right on Route 537 (Monmouth Road).**

Use caution, high speed traffic.

**2.6   Right on Route 669 (Juliustown Road).**

**2.7   Stop. Flashing red light. Continue straight at intersection with Route 206, still on Route 669.**

This road goes by an area of farms. Arney's Mount is visible straight ahead. You start up the hill at 4.0 miles.

At 230 feet, Arney's Mount is part of the low ridge which separates the Inner and Outer Coastal plains. The area to the north and west of this ridge slopes toward the Delaware River. The area to the southeast slopes toward the Atlantic Ocean. In general the soil in the Inner Coastal Plain is more fertile and less sandy than the soil of the Outer Coastal Plain.

**4.8   Continue straight at intersection with Arney's Mount Road, still on Route 669.**

The Arney's Mount Meeting House, built in 1775, is on the right at this intersection.

This part of New Jersey was settled in a west to east direction. Early settlers, English Quakers, reached present day Burlington in 1677 and moved east across the county. (Burlington County was established in 1681). The establishment of agriculture was limited east of here, when set-

**To prove the stability of the Star Bicycle, manufactured in Smithville, a rider rode it down the Capitol steps.**

tlers reached the Pine Barrens.

**6.2** **Four-way stop. Left on Route 663 (Juliustown and Georgetown Road).**

**7.5** **Stop. Continue straight at intersection with Saylors Pond Road, still on Route 663.**

Cross small bridge at 7.6 miles.

**8.3** **Stop. Right on Springfield Meeting House Road.**

More horse farms line this scenic road.

**9.7** **Stop. Continue straight at intersection with Route 68, still on Springfield Meeting House Road.**

Shift to low gear as you go up this short steep hill.

**9.9** **Stop. Left on Highland Road. Road becomes dirt/gravel after a short distance.**

The Upper Springfield Meeting House and Burial Ground is on the left at this intersection. The early 18th-century meeting house is one of the oldest in New Jersey. A marker describes its history.

A short distance to the right along this road is downtown Wrightstown. Near Wrightstown at the edge of the Pinelands National Reserve, are Maguire Air Force Base and Fort Dix Military Reservation.

A small wildlife preserve is on the left after the meeting house.

**11.1** **Stop. Right on Route 537 (Monmouth Road). Use caution, high speed traffic.**

A farm market is at this intersection.

**11.3** **Traffic light. Left on Route 545 (Georgetown-Wrightsville Road). Use caution, high speed traffic.**

A diner and convenience store are at this intersection, and a large horse farm on the right at 12.0 miles.

**12.8** **Bear to right at junction with Route 68, still on Route 545.**

**13.3** **Bear right on Georgetown-Chesterfield Road.**

The small settlement of Georgetown dates from the 18th-century and is named for Congessman George Sykes.

**15.8** **Stop. Continue straight, now on Route 667 (Chesterfield-Crosswicks Road).**

Chesterfield was formerly called Recklesstown. The Chesterfield Inn is on the right.

**17.3 Bear to right slightly at intersection with Margerum Road, now on Route 660 (Crosswicks Road).**

This road enters Crosswicks at 18.0 miles. Crosswicks is one of the best preserved 18th-century towns in New Jersey. A ride through the town's well-maintained streets is a real pleasure.

**18.3 Left on Front Street. This is the street just before the stop sign.**

There is a restaurant just beyond this intersection and a deli one block to the left on Main Street.

**18.5 Right on Church Street.**

The Crosswicks Meeting House, built in 1773, replaced an earlier structure from 1706. Walk around the building and look for the small cannonball that is lodged in one of its walls. It dates from 1778 and a small skirmish during the Revolutionary War.

**18.6 Stop. Left on Route 660.**

The Chesterfield Historical Society is on the right as you leave town.

At 19.3 miles the road crosses over the New Jersey Turnpike. The New Jersey State Reformatory is located to the right.

**20.5 Left on Hogback Avenue (sign is hard to read).**

**21.2 Stop. Left on Route 528.**

Recross the turnpike at 21.4 miles.

**22.5 Right on Route 660 (Old York Road).**

**23.9 Stop. Left on Route 545 (Bordentown-Georgetown Road).**

Look for the wooded area as you cross a small bridge over Blacks Creek at 24.7 miles.

**25.2 Right on White Pine Road (dirt/gravel road for a short section).**

Kuser pond is to the left as you ride through this wooded area. Across the small bridge at 25.8 miles, the road becomes paved.

**26.3 Stop. Continue straight at intersection with Route 68, still on White Pine Road. Use caution crossing Route 68.**

**26.9 Left on North Island Road.**

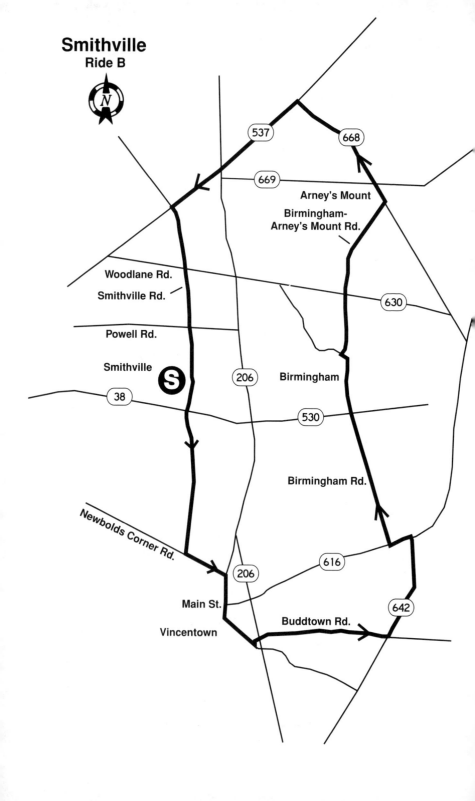

# Smithville
## Ride B

N

537    668

669

Arney's Mount

Birmingham-
Arney's Mount Rd.

Woodlane Rd.

Smithville Rd.

630

Powell Rd.

Smithville    **S**

206    Birmingham

38

530

Birmingham Rd.

Newbolds Corner Rd.

206    616

Main St.    642

Vincentown    Buddtown Rd.

**27.8 Stop. Right on Mansfield Road.**

**27.9 Left on Island Road.**

There are woods and old houses to enjoy before the road goes through a development.

**29.1 Stop. Right on Route 543 (Columbus Road). It becomes East Main Street in Columbus.**

**30.0 Flashing yellow light. Continue straight on East Main Street at intersection with New York Road.**

A general store is located at this intersection. At 30.1 miles the road crosses over Route 206.

**31.6 Left on Route 628 (Jacksonville Road).**

Cross small bridge over Assicunk Creek at 32.5 miles.

**33.3 Traffic light. Continue straight at intersection with Route 528, still on Route 628.**

**33.5 Left on Jacksonville-Smithville Road.**

**33.6 Right, still on Jacksonville-Smithville Road.**

**36.2 Traffic light. Continue straight at intersection with Route 537, still on Jacksonville-Smithville Road.**

**37.0 Traffic light. Continue straight at intersection with Route 630 (Woodlane Road), now on Smithville Road.**

**37.7 Stop. Continue straight at intersection with Powell Road, still on Smithville Road.**

**37.9 Right on Mead Lane at park entrance. End of tour.**

## Directions: Ride B

**0.0  Right on Smithville Road.**

The road crosses over Rancocas Creek at 0.2 mile. Smithville Lake is to the right. Before Hezekiah Smith purchased this area, it was known as Shreveville and a large cotton mill was located here.

**0.9  Stop. Continue straight (a little to left) across Route 38, still on Smithville Road. Use caution, heavy traffic on Route 38.**

This paved road is a little rough in sections.

**2.5  Stop. Left on Newbolds Corner Road (unmarked).**

**3.1**  **Stop. Right on Route 681 (Main Street).**

Downtown Vincentown offers some antique shops, a cafe and a pizza shop.

**4.3**  **Left on Buddtown Road (last road before traffic light).**

**4.4**  **Stop. Continue straight at intersection with Route 206, still on Buddtown Road. Use caution crossing Route 206.**

This road enters into the Pinelands National Reserve. Although in the 19th century it was mostly pine forest, it is now mostly farmland.

**6.0**  **Stop. Left on Route 642 (Ridge Road).**

The small collection of houses you come upon is Buddtown.

**7.3**  **Stop. Left on Route 616 (Pemberton Road).**

**7.6**  **Right on Birmingham Road.**

The road can be rough in spots. At 7.7 miles cross a little bridge.

**9.2**  **Stop. Continue straight across Route 530, still on Birmingham Road.**

**9.9**  **Bear right after crossing the bridge over Rancocas Creek, now on Birmingham-Arney's Mount Road (unmarked).**

Birmingham Forge was located on the Rancocas Creek in the early 1800s.

**10.7**  **Stop. Continue straight across Route 630, still on Birmingham-Arney's Mount Road.**

This road goes up Arney's Mount. Shift to low gear as you go up one of the few substantial climbs among all the tours in this book.

**12.6**  **Stop. Left on Route 668 (Arney's Mount-Pemberton Road).**

**12.9**  **Stop. Continue straight at intersection with Route 669, still on Route 668.**

The Arney's Mount Friends Meeting House is to the left at this intersection.

**14.3**  **Stop. Left on Route 537. Use caution, high speed traffic.**

Magnolia Manor c. 1790, which is a private residence, is at 14.3 miles.

**14.8**  **Traffic light. Continue straight at Route 206, still on Route 537.**

**15.5** Traffic light. Left on Smithville Road.

**16.4** Traffic light. Continue straight at intersection with Woodlane Road, still on Smithville Road.

**17.1** Traffic light. Continue straight at intersection with Powell Road, still on Smithville Road.

**17.3** Right on Mead Lane at park entrance. End of tour.

"Old Barney" is one of the most recognizable symbols of the Jersey Shore.

# Ocean and Monmouth Counties

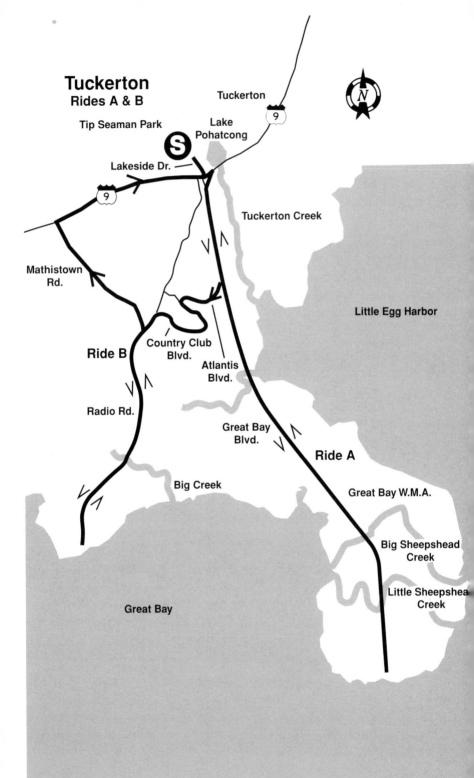

# Tuckerton
## Rides A & B

Tuckerton

Tip Seaman Park

Lake Pohatcong

S

Lakeside Dr.

9

Tuckerton Creek

Little Egg Harbor

Mathistown Rd.

Ride B

Country Club Blvd.

Atlantis Blvd.

Radio Rd.

Great Bay Blvd.

Ride A

Big Creek

Great Bay W.M.A.

Big Sheepshead Creek

Little Sheepshead Creek

Great Bay

# *Tuckerton*

## *Start:*

Tip Seaman County Park, Tuckerton, Ocean County. Garden State Parkway Exit 58 east to downtown Tuckerton. Turn right at traffic light on Route 9. Turn right on Lakeside Drive south of Lake Pohatcong to parking at Tip Seaman Park.

## *Rides:*

**Ride A** is 13.3 miles on paved roads with light to moderate traffic. The end of Great Bay Boulevard is very rough ending in a short gravel section.

**Ride B** is 13.4 miles on paved roads with light to moderate traffic. The rides can be easily combined into a 23.9 mile ride by riding Ride A first, then riding Ride B starting at Atlantis Boulevard.

If you don't know the difference between a cherrystone and a little neck, or a ring-necked duck and a scaup, or a garvey and a sneakbox you can learn in Tuckerton. The Barnegat Bay Decoy and Baymen's Museum has exhibits, tools and artifacts pertaining to the life of the bayman. Soon it will be joined by the Tuckerton Seaport: A Maritime Cultural Center. This complex will eventually have 26 buildings dedicated to preserving the area's history and educating the public about the past, present and future of the Barnegat Bay.

The Barnegat Bay and Little Egg Harbor waterway is 40 miles long with a width of one to four miles. It is a mixture of salt and freshwater, with most of the bay less than six feet in depth at low tide. For centuries this unique environment has provided man with food and a livelihood. Native Americans clammed and fished these waters for centuries before the first Europeans arrived. From the early 1700s through the 1950s many local men earned their living on the bay by clamming, oystering, fishing and hunting. However, because of overdevelopment, pollution and over-harvesting there are now few people who make their entire livelihood off the bay. Today more decoys end up on collectors' shelves rather than floating on the bay.

Tuckerton was the most important town on the bay in the 18th and 19th centuries. During the Revolutionary War, as many as 30 privateers used the town to unload cargo from captured ships. In 1791 George Washington named Tuckerton America's third port of entry after New York and Philadelphia. With the establishment of a railroad line in 1871, it became a popular destination for vacationers, who were then ferried on the steamboats *Barclay* and *Pohatcong* to resorts on Long Beach Island. When the Tuckerton Seaport is finished, it is hoped the town will once again become a tourist destination. Already more than 40,000 people come here in September for the annual Old Time Barnegat Bay Decoy and Gunning Show (see calendar for more information).

Ride A goes out Great Bay Boulevard to the Great Bay Wildlife Management Area. There are views of Little Egg Inlet and Long Beach Island. Ride B goes out Radio Road past the location of a Revolutionary War massacre. At the end of this road are views of Atlantic City and Great Bay.

(By the way, a cherrystone clam is larger than a little-neck clam. A garvey is a scowlike workboat, and a sneak-box is a small hunting boat. The ring neck duck has a distictive ringed bill: the scaup, a plain bill.)

## *Directions: Ride A*

### 0.0   Exit Tip Seaman Park to left onto Route 9.

You'll find the Barnegat Bay Decoy and Baymen's Museum to the right as you exit the park. The building is a reproduction of a hunting shanty.

### 0.1   Right on Great Bay Boulevard.

Just past this intersection, to the right, is the future home of the Tuckerton Seaport. Tuckerton, which had been known as Middle-of-the-Shore, Quakertown, Fishtown and Clamtown, was given its current name in the 1780s to honor its most prominent citizen, Judge Ebenezer Tucker.

Stewart's (also located just beyond the intersection) is a good place to get some food before or after your ride. Although you won't be able to take advantage of the 1950s style carhop service, you can sit at a picnic table and enjoy a root beer and burger.

Tuckerton Creek is to the left and Holly Lake is to the right as you ride through this residential area.

**1.4 Intersection with Atlantis Boulevard to right (sign for Atlantis Golf Course). Ride B turn.**

**2.4 Cross bridge over Big Thorofare Creek. Enter Great Bay Wildlife Management Area.**

There is a marina to the right.

**3.2 Cross bridge over Little Thorofare Creek.**

Look for two more marinas along this part of Great Bay Boulevard. You can get soda and snacks at both. First Bridge County Park is located at this point.

Little Egg Harbor and Tuckerton Bay are located to the left. Dutch Captain Cornelius Mey named the area while exploring the coast in 1614. Thousands of meadowbird eggs were piled on the shore at the mouths of two rivers. He named them the Little Egg Harbor River (now the Mullica) and the Great Egg Harbor River.

**4.9 Traffic light. Straight across bridge over Big Sheepshead Creek. Use caution—this is a very narrow wooden bridge.**

Stay to center if fishermen and crabbers are using the edge walkways. At 5.4 miles the pavement gets very rough.

**5.8 Traffic light. Straight across bridge over Little Sheepshead Creek. Use caution—narrow wooden bridge.**

At 6.3 miles the rough pavement gives way to smoother gravel. This is a great area for bird watching. Look for the Osprey *(Pandion haliaetus)* nest on the platform to the right. Snowy Egrets *(Egretta thula)* often wade in the shallow marsh areas.

**6.6 Stop. End of road. Return to Tuckerton on Great Bay Boulevard.**

There is a short trail to the bay edge (watch out for flies).

**13.2 Stop. Left on Route 9.**

**13.3 Right into Tip Seaman Park. End of tour.**

# Directions: Ride B

Follow directions for Ride A to 1.4 miles. Turn right on Atlantis Boulevard (sign for Atlantis Golf Course).

**2.1  Stop. Left on Country Club Boulevard (unmarked).**

There are views of water to the left as this road circles the golf course.

**3.3  Stop. Left on Radio Road.**

This road goes through the center of the Mystic Islands housing development.

**3.5  Traffic light. Continue straight through intersection with Mathistown Road.**

Just south of the intersection, on Kosciusko Way, is a monument to the colonists killed October 15, 1777. As part of the same action that destroyed Chestnut Neck (see Edwin B. Forsythe-Port Republic section), British and Loyalist soldiers landed on Osborne Island and marched toward Tuckerton to destroy it and its privateers. The colonists had been warned and no privateers remained in the harbor. A force under Count Pulaski, which had arrived from Trenton, was encamped on this road to defend the town. However, they were surprised by the British and about 30 were killed, some while they slept. When the main body of colonists was aroused, the British retreated down this road toward their ships.[20]

Radio Road continues through a shopping and residential area. Much of this area was formerly wetlands, filled in later for the housing development.

**5.2  Straight across bridge over Big Creek.**

As the British retreated they tore up the planks on the bridge that was located here, preventing the colonists from pursuing. The Forsythe Wildlife Refuge lies to the right along part of this road.

**6.6  End of road. Turn around and return on Radio Road.**

There are views of Atlantic City and Great Bay. The mouth of the Mullica River is to the right.

In 1912, a German radio company started construction of what was then one of the tallest structures in the world. Completed in 1914, the radio tower stood over 850 feet tall. The U.S. government seized the tower during WWI when it was suspected of being used by the Germans to transmit data about shipping. Some suspected it was used in the sinking of the Lusitania, although this was never proved. Dismantled years ago, only some of the tower's concrete piers still remain, along with the road's name.

**9.6  Traffic Light. Left on Mathistown Road.**

**10.1 Traffic light. Continue straight through intersection with Center Street, still on Mathistown.**

**11.3 Traffic light. Right on Route 9.**

There is a convenience store and an ice cream stand at 12.6 miles, where Route 9 enters Tuckerton.

**12.8 Traffic light. Continue straight through intersection with Oak Lane, still on Route 9.**

**13.4 Left into Tip Seaman Park. End of tour.**

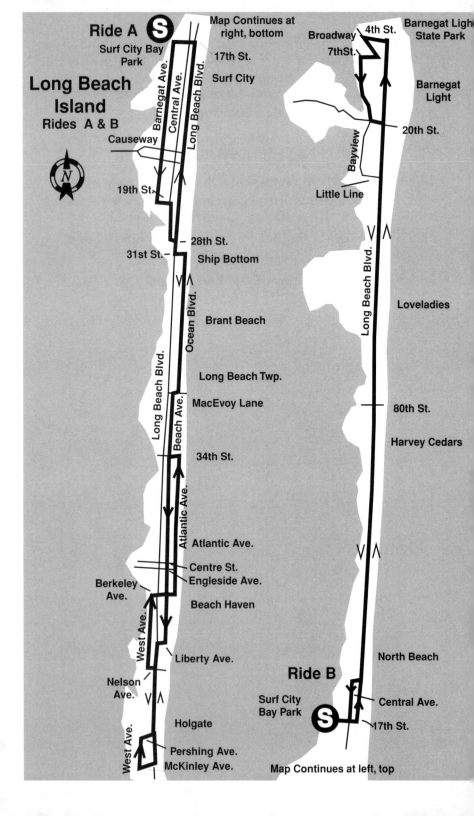

Ride A S

Long Beach Island
Rides A & B

N

Surf City Bay Park

Barnegat Ave.

Central Ave.

Long Beach Blvd.

Map Continues at right, bottom

17th St.

Surf City

Causeway

19th St.

28th St.

31st St.

Ship Bottom

Ocean Blvd.

Brant Beach

Long Beach Blvd.

Long Beach Twp.

Beach Ave.

MacEvoy Lane

34th St.

Atlantic Ave.

Atlantic Ave.

Centre St.

Engleside Ave.

Berkeley Ave.

Beach Haven

West Ave.

Liberty Ave.

Nelson Ave.

Holgate

West Ave.

Pershing Ave.

McKinley Ave.

Broadway

4th St.

Barnegat Light State Park

7th St.

Barnegat Light

Bayview

20th St.

Little Line

Long Beach Blvd.

Loveladies

80th St.

Harvey Cedars

North Beach

Ride B

Surf City Bay Park

S

Central Ave.

17th St.

Map Continues at left, top

# Long Beach Island

## Start:

Surf City Bay Park, Surf City, Ocean County. Route 72 over Long Beach Island Causeway to traffic light at Barnegat Avenue. Left on Barnegat Avenue 1.1 miles to Surf City Bay Park on left. Parking available on Barnegat Avenue adjacent to park.

## Rides:

**Ride A** is 22.7 miles on paved roads with moderate to heavy traffic (summer).

**Ride B** is 17.1 miles on paved roads with light to moderate traffic (heavy in summer). The rides can be easily combined, resulting in a 39.8 mile tour.

In the 19th century, shipwrecks were a common occurrence along the New Jersey coast. The 20 mile stretch along Long Beach Island was one of the most dangerous. Between 1840 and 1880, well over 100 ships were driven aground by storms. Trapped a few hundred yards offshore, most crews and passengers were unable to reach shore because of stormy seas and frigid temperatures. In 1847, a series of refuge houses were constructed at 20-mile intervals along the coast. These rudimentary shelters were manned by volunteers and contained rescue equipment and basic supplies. But they proved to be only partially successful in saving lives. In 1854 the *Powhatan* grounded off Surf City and volunteers were unable to reach the ship before it capsized with a loss of 350 lives.[21]

It took until 1871 to improve the system. In this year the United States Life Saving Service was formed. New larger buildings were constructed, placed only three miles apart, and manned by professional crews from September through April. Countless lives were saved by these men until the 1890s when the era of the steamship arrived and wrecks became much less frequent. Long Beach Island had six stations, of which three still remain.

Besides going by these stations in Beach Haven

Terrace, Harvey Cedars and Loveladies, these rides connect a number of other interesting sites on the island. Ride A goes south through Ship Bottom, Long Beach Township and Beach Haven. Here you can visit the Long Beach Island Historical Museum and tour the town's Victorian district. It continues to Holgate where you can park your bike and take a hike at the Edwin Forsythe National Wildlife Refuge. Ride B goes north through the less populated section of the island to Barnegat Light State Park, where you can climb the 217 steps to the top of Barnegat Lighthouse.

Long Beach Island was my home for a number of years. During the last 15 years I have ridden the length of the island well over a hundred times. The routes I have outlined are just two of the many ways to tour the island while avoiding as much traffic as possible. However, between Memorial Day and Labor Day there is no way to avoid the crowds. Another hint: if you have the option, start by riding into the wind and using the tailwind to carry you back.

## *Directions: Ride A*

**0.0  Exit park south on Barnegat Avenue. (The park is to your right).**

Barnegat Avenue is wide with a good biking shoulder.

**1.1  Traffic light. Continue straight across Causeway inbound and outbound lanes (8th and 9th Streets).**

**1.7  Left on 19th Street.**

**1.9  Stop. Right on Central Avenue. Continue straight through the next traffic light.**

Pass the crabbing and fishing pavilion on the right as you pedal through Ship Bottom.

**2.4  Left on 28th Street.**

**2.4  Traffic light. Right on Long Beach Boulevard.**

**2.6  Left on 31st Street. Use caution crossing Long Beach Boulevard.**

If you don't want to cross here, you can continue down Long Beach Boulevard and turn at one of the following traffic lights.

**2.7  Right on Ocean Boulevard (also known as "the Beach Road"). Watch for other cyclists, in-line skaters and pedestrians.**

This two-lane road is much more relaxing than Long Beach Boulevard, plus there are no traffic lights to interrupt your rhythm. As you continue through Long Beach Township, watch for pedestrians crossing on every side street on their way to or from the beach.

**6.3  Stop. Right on MacEvoy Lane.**

**6.3  Left on Beach Avenue.**

The Beach Haven Terrace Life Saving Station, which became the Coast Guard station, is located one block to the left on Maryland Avenue. Look for the red and white building with the four-story tower.

**7.9  Four-way stop. Continue straight at intersection with Twelfth Avenue, still on Beach Avenue. This is now a one-way road. Continue straight through series of four-way stops as you ride through Beach Haven.**

At 8.4 miles on the left, on the corner of Third Street, is the Beach Haven Public Library, a pretty little building that was dedicated in 1924. It has a small museum with items relating to the early days of Beach Haven.

**8.5  Four-way stop. Continue straight at intersection with Centre Street, still on Beach Avenue.**

The Show Place is a great place to stop for ice cream.

**8.6  Four-way stop. Continue straight at Engleside Avenue, still on Beach Avenue.**

On this corner is the Long Beach Island Historical Association Museum. The building was once Holy Innocents Episcopal Church, the island's first church, built in 1882. Call (609) 492-0700 for more information and hours.

Here is the center of Beach Haven's historic Victorian district. There are many interesting private residences and a few bed and breakfasts along the adjoining side streets.

**8.9  Four-way stop. Continue straight at Berkeley Avenue, still on Beach Avenue.**

**9.3  Right on Liberty Avenue, as Beach Avenue ends.**

**9.5  Stop. Left on Bay Avenue. (Long Beach Boulevard).**

There is a wide bike lane and this section of Long Beach Boulevard is much less busy than farther north.

A bike rental shop and some small stores appear along this road as you continue south into Holgate.

**11.0 Right on McKinley Avenue, as Bay Avenue ends.**

The island extends two miles south of this point. It is part of the Edwin Forsythe National Wildlife Refuge. If you have the time, lock your bike at the parking area and take a hike on the beach.

The southern end of the refuge is closed to all people April–September to protect endangered Piping Plover nesting sites on the beach.

**11.1 Stop. Right on West Avenue.**

Continue past the only trailer park on the island.

**11.3 Right on Pershing Avenue.**

**11.5 Stop. Left on Bay Avenue.**

If you have a tail wind, you can pick up some speed on this mile stretch.

**12.5 Left on Nelson Avenue.**

**12.6 Right on West Avenue.**

**The bicycle is the best way to get to the beach on Long Beach Island.**

There are views of the bay as you continue past the Beach Haven Coast Guard Station at 12.9 miles.

**13.4 Right on Berkeley Avenue.**

The Little Egg Harbor Yacht Club is alongside the bay at this intersection.

**13.6 Traffic light. Continue straight across Bay Avenue, still on Berkeley Avenue.**

**13.7 Four-way stop. Continue straight across Beach Avenue still on Berkeley Avenue.**

**13.8 Stop. Left on Atlantic Avenue (one-way). Continue through four-way stops, staying on Atlantic Avenue. Two-way traffic after a mile.**

Although Long Beach Island is one of the few shore areas in New Jersey without a boardwalk, there was one in Beach Haven until 1944, when it was destroyed by a hurricane. It ran from 7th Street south to Holyoke Avenue.

You pass by some oceanfront motels as you ride along the ocean through Beach Haven.

**15.7 Stop. Left on 34th Street.**

**15.8 Stop. Right on Beach Avenue.**

**16.3 Stop. Right on MacEvoy Lane.**

**16.4 Left on Ocean Boulevard/Beach Avenue.**

Retrace the route through Long Beach Township.

**19.9 Stop. Left on 31st Street.**

**20.0 Stop. Right on Long Beach Boulevard.**

Use caution as you continue through a series of traffic lights in Ship Bottom.

**21.2 Continue straight at Causeway intersection. Use caution and watch for merging and turning traffic. Continue through a series of traffic lights through Surf City.**

Surf City, near the location of present day 7th Street, was the location of the aforementioned wreck of the *Powhatan* on April 16, 1854.

There is a bike shop on the right at 21.4 miles and a number of other stores and restaurants in Surf City.

**22.4 Left on 17th Street. Continue straight at stop signs at Central Avenue and Sunset Avenue.**

**22.7** Bear to left on Barnegat Avenue.

**22.7** Surf City Bay Park on left. End of tour.

## *Directions: Ride B.*

**0.0** Exit parking north on Barnegat Avenue. Road bends immediately away from the bay, now on 17th Street. Continue straight at stop signs at Sunset Avenue and Central Avenue.

Long Beach Island's first residents were whalers who came from New England in the 1690s. Hundreds of acres of white cedar bogs and thick undergrowth covered the area, which became known as the Great Swamp. The settlers used the tall cedars as lookouts for whales, that swam along the coast. Both the swamp and trees were leveled by a hurricane in 1821.

**0.3** Stop. Left on Long Beach Boulevard. Continue through traffic lights in Surf City and Harvey Cedars as you ride north toward Barnegat Light.

The road varies from four-lane to two-lane.

After leaving Surf City, you ride through North Beach which is a part of Long Beach Township. Up until about 1950, this was undeveloped and the state considered purchasing a large tract of land here for an oceanfront park.

The island narrows even further as you enter Harvey Cedars. At the intersection of Cape May Avenue is the Long Beach Island Fishing Club, which occupies the former Harvey Cedars Life Saving Station. Look for the cedar shingled building with the tower.

If you want to see the only remaining old hotel on the island, turn left at the traffic light at Camden Avenue in Harvey Cedars. Now the Harvey Cedars Bible Conference, this building was originally called the Connahassett House and later the Harvey Cedars Hotel.

The name Harvey Cedars derives from "harvest cedars", a reference to a high place in the bay where men could camp while harvesting salt hay.

At 3.2 miles on the left is Maris Stella. Formerly a private estate, it is now owned by the Sisters of Charity.

Loveladies, which you enter at 4.0 miles, is named for Thomas Lovelady of Waretown who owned a nearby island in Barnegat Bay. This tract of land had previously been known as Club House for a local hotel. Except for a few shacks and the hotel, which was later abandoned, this land remained largely undeveloped until the late 1950s. Loveladies, like North Beach, is a part of Long Beach Township. Look for the Loveladies Life Saving Station on the boulevard across from the Long Beach Arts and Sciences building.

After passing 30th Street, you enter Barnegat Light, where Long Beach Boulevard is called Central Avenue. On the corner of 7th Street and Central Avenue look for the small church called St. Peters at the Light. It was built in the 1890s by a boatwright. On Central Avenue and 5th Street is the Barnegat Light Museum and Edith Duff Gardens. Call (609) 494-8578 for information and hours.

**8.3  Bear left on 4th Street, at end of Central Avenue.**

There are a number of older cottages in the shadow of the lighthouse.

**8.5  Stop. Right on Broadway.**

**8.6  Barnegat Lighthouse State Park is on the right. The inlet and a view of Island Beach State Park are straight ahead. After visit return via Broadway.**

Barnegat Lighthouse was built in the late 1850s to replace an earlier structure that toppled into the sea. Its construction was overseen by George Meade, who commanded the Union forces at Gettysburg a few years later. "Old Barney" probably rivals the boardwalk as the symbol of the Jersey Shore.

If you want to take a break before starting back, there are ice cream shops and restaurants along Broadway.

**8.8  Right on 7th street.**

**9.0  Stop. Left on Bayview Avenue.**

The Barnegat Light Coast Guard Station is along the bay to the right. As you continue you pass the commercial fishing docks, which are some of the most active in New Jersey.

**9.8  Four-way stop. Left on 20th Street.**

**9.9  Stop. Right on Long Beach Boulevard. Once again continue straight through traffic lights as you return to Surf City.**

At 15.2 miles the highway divides. The 1899 sign at the entrance to North Beach, refers to the year Long Beach Township was formed, not when settlement started.

**16.5** **Right on 24th Street, at sign for Route 72, Manahawkin and Beach Haven.**

**16.5** **Bear left on Central Avenue, yield to merging traffic on right.**

**16.8** **Continue straight at intersection with 19th Street, still on Central Avenue.**

**16.9** **Right on 17th street.**

**17.0** **Continue straight across Sunset Avenue (unmarked), still on 17th Street.**

**17.1** **Bear left on Barnegat Avenue.**

**17.1** **Surf City Bay Park on right. End of tour.**

A Pitch Pine "corkscrews" into the sky near Waretown, Ocean County.

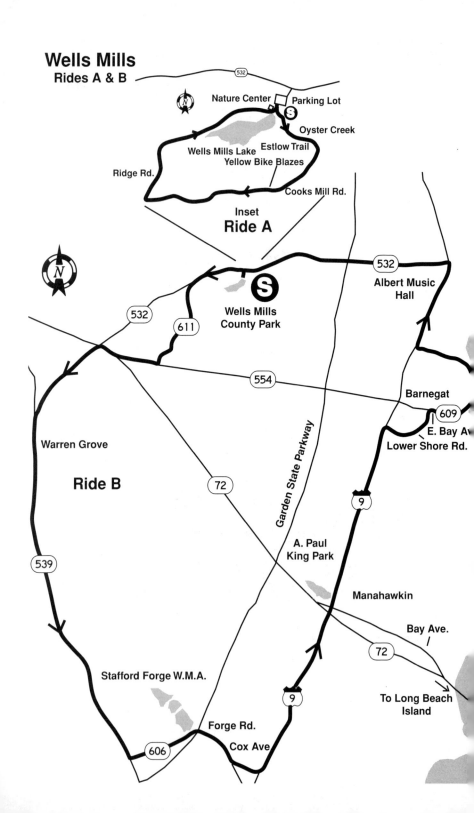

# *Wells Mills*

## *Start:*

Wells Mills County Park, Waretown, Ocean County. Garden State Parkway North to Exit 69. Turn left on Route 532 west and continue two miles to park entrance on left. Garden State Parkway South to Exit 67. Turn right (west) on Route 554 and proceed for 3.5 miles to Route 611 (Brookeville Road). Turn right and go 1.8 miles to Route 532. Turn right on Route 532 and proceed to park entrance on right.

## *Rides:*

**Ride A** is 3.0 miles on a dirt/sand road and a narrow forest trail.

**Ride B** is 33.9 miles on paved roads with light to heavy (Route 9 through Manahawkin) traffic.

Two of the most important pinelands products were the Atlantic White Cedar *(Chamaecyparis thyoides)* and the sphagnum mosses (20 identified species including *S. magellanicum, S. fallax,* and *S. cuspidatum.*). Both of these thrive in wet lowland areas, including streams and along the natural bogs commonly referred to as "cedar swamps." Along the edge of these wetlands the cedars grow in thick rows. With their straight tall trunks, they are one of the most recognizable trees in the Pine Barrens. Covering their roots and fanning out across the surrounding water are thick mats of sphagnum moss. At the mat edges stems rise up in unique star clusters.

Early settlers, perhaps following the lead of Native Americans, soon discovered uses for both these products. The tall Atlantic White Cedar, rot-resistant and relatively knot-free, became favored for shingles, fences and shipbuilding. In the 19th century, there were dozens of sawmills dedicated to the harvest and processing of this tree. One of the largest, longest running sawmills was located at Wells Mills. James Wells established the first sawmill at this location after the Revolutionary War, on land seized from a Tory. In the 1870s another owner built a second sawmill next to the first (thus the plural name of the park today). Operations continued until 1940 when the land became a private recreational retreat.

One of the ancillary occupations of local settlers was the gathering of sphagnum moss. This moss is one of the most absorbent plant products known. It is said that Native-Americans used it for diapers. Settlers used it as a poultice because it contains an anti-bacterial agent. Indeed, it was used by the United States Army in World War I for treating wounds. With the development of the landscape and floral business at the turn of the 20th century, sphagnum became the preferred product for packing plants because of its ability to hold water. Even with the development of artificial products, it is still used today for this purpose and there are still a few people in the Pine Barrens who practice this trade.

Wells Mills was acquired by the state starting in the 1970s. It now contains 900 acres and is one of the most diverse smaller parks in the entire Pine Barrens. Ride A is a short off-road ride going through lowlands and uplands within the park. Ride B leaves the park and goes through the heart of southern Ocean County. Wells Mills hosts the Pine Barrens Jamboree every October. This popular festival features Pine Barrens music, food and crafts. Call (609) 971-3085 for more information.

## *Directions: Ride A*

**0.0  Trail mileage starts at bulletin board/map adjacent to parking lot. Sign in at booklet here. Continue down path toward nature center. Bear left at nature center toward lake.**

For the most part the bike trail follows Ridge Road and Cooks Mill Road (two historic Pine Barrens roads). Whenever possible follow Yellow Bike Blazes.

The Nature Center has an exhibit area on Pine Barrens ecology. Park literature and trail maps are available here.

**0.1  At junction of Pink Blazes, Green Blazes and White Blazes, stay to right following White and Green Blazes.**

**0.2  Cross bridge over Oyster Creek.**

As the road bends away from the lake you enter an area of thick sugar sand. You climb, almost imperceptibly into an uplands area of Pitch Pines. Yellow Bike Blazes begin to appear.

**1.5 Right at Yellow Bike Blaze (In fork between paths).**

You will go downhill to small bridge over a wetlands area. The path narrows to shoulder width.

**1.8 Right at sign for private scout reservation.**

Continue straight, as footpaths join and leave main path.

**2.0 Long walkway. Use caution, can be slippery.**

At about 2.4 the trail widens. Look for mushrooms along this section.

**2.8 Cross small bridge over Field Branch.**

**3.0 Trail ends as you emerge from the woods just west of the nature center. End of tour.**

To your right is Wells Mills Lake. Next to the lake is the cabin built in 1937 by the Conrads, owners of the property at that time.

## Directions: Ride B

**0.0 Exit park to the left on Route 532 (Wells Mills Road).**

**1.3 Left on Route 611 (Brookeville Road). Look for the sign for the scout camps.**

Brookeville, believe it or not, was one of the larger towns for many miles in the 19th century. Children walked here from miles around to attend the area's one- room schoolhouse. The Methodist Church dates from 1850.

**3.1 Stop. Right on 554 west (Straight Road).**

**4.0 Yield. Straight onto Route 72.**

**4.4 Left on Route 532 (Warren Grove Road). Use caution crossing Route 72.**

This rolling road goes through a mixed oak and pine forest.

**6.5 Stop. Left on Route 539.**

To the right is the pygmy forest (see Penn State Forest-Chatsworth section). Two government facilities are also located here. They are a government aeronautical communications station and, as you continue further, a weapons range that occupies approximately 8500 acres.

Warren Grove supposedly got its name from General Joseph Warren who was killed in the Revolutionary War. Lucille's Country Cooking in Warren Grove is a good place to stop for food. There are scenic views along this road as the pines slope in front of you toward the coast.

The road continues through portions of the Stafford Forge Wildlife Management Area and Bass River State Forest.

**13.5 Left on Route 606 (Forge Road). This unmarked road is the last before crossing the parkway.**

At 14.7 miles is one of the entrances to Stafford Forge Wildlife Management Area and Stafford Forge Lake. Stafford Forge operated at this location from the 1790s through 1840. There are a number of trails through here that are good for off-road riding.

Continue under the parkway at 15.0 miles.

**15.9 Left on Cox Ave.**

**16.6 Stop. Left on Route 9. Use caution—moderate high speed traffic. Good shoulder.**

There are a number of small stores and produce stands along this road, and a bike shop on the left as you enter Cedar Run.

**19.1 Continue straight at junction with Route 72. Use caution as traffic merges and exits.**

**19.3 Traffic light. Continue straight through intersection with Bay Avenue. Continue through traffic lights at 20.2 and 20.5 miles in Manahawkin.**

There is a fair amount of traffic but a good shoulder.

A. Paul King Park is to the left at this intersection. Swimming is allowed in season and there are picnic benches and public restrooms — altogether a good place for a ride break.

Adjacent to the park is The Old Stone Store which dates from 1838. Manahawkin is an Indian name that has been interpreted as meaning "good corn land." Stafford Township's original settlers came from Staffordshire in England. James Haywood, Perry Paul and Luke Courtney purchased land in 1735 and settled in 1743.

**23.2 Right on Lower Shore Road.**

**23.8 Bear left, still on Lower Shore Road.**

**24.5 Stop. Right on Route 609 (E. Bay Avenue).**

The Barnegat Historical Society Museum is to your right as you continue down this road. Barnegat is derived from the Dutch Barende-gat meaning "inlet of breakers."

**25.1 Cross small bridge over Double Creek, now on Bay Shore Drive.**

To the right is a portion of the Edwin B. Forsythe National Wildlife Refuge. Across Barnegat Bay is Long Beach Island and to the north, Island Beach State Park. Although Island Beach isn't included in this book, it's a great place to ride. The park is reached via Route 37 to south on Route 35. It's a simple 16-mile out-and-back ride on the park's only road.

The little park to the right has public restrooms and a pavilion overlooking the bay. Follow the road as it bends away from the bay through a residential area.

**27.6 Traffic light. Right on Route 9.**

There are some stores at this intersection.

**29.5 Traffic light. Left on Route 532 (sign for Warren Grove).**

According to Henry Charlton Beck in *Forgotten Towns of Southern New Jersey*, Waretown was the headquarters of the Rogerines for a short time in the middle of the 1700s. The Rogerines were a persecuted religious sect who believed in adult baptism and non-observance of the Sabbath. Their habit of heckling preachers of other faiths did not endear them to the local populace.[22]

At 29.9 miles is the newly-constructed Albert Music Hall. Every Saturday night at 7:30 P.M. there are concerts. Music has been an important part of Pine Barrens culture since earliest settlement. Isolated from more populated areas, settlers relied on dance and music halls as the center of social activity. Although similar to other rural music including bluegrass, the isolation within which it developed has made it unique. Of particular interest are lyrics that focus on the history and environment of the bay and pines. The hall is named for Joe Albert who, with his brother George, started the "Home Place" in the 1950s. It became a place for local musicians to gather on Saturday night for impromptu concerts. There is a small admission charge.

The road has rolling hills with pines on both sides. You cross the parkway at 31.6 miles and a small bridge at 32.5 miles.

**33.9 Park entrance on left. End of tour.**

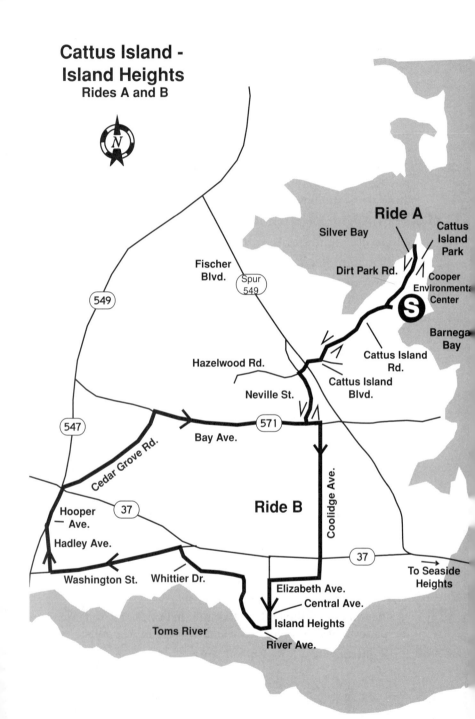

# Cattus Island -
# Island Heights
### Rides A and B

*N*

Ride A

Silver Bay

Cattus Island Park

Fischer Blvd.

Spur 549

Dirt Park Rd.

Cooper Environmental Center

549

Cattus Island Rd.

Barnegat Bay

Hazelwood Rd.

Cattus Island Blvd.

Neville St.

571

547

Bay Ave.

Cedar Grove Rd.

Ride B

Coolidge Ave.

37

Hooper Ave.

Hadley Ave.

37

To Seaside Heights

Washington St.

Whittier Dr.

Elizabeth Ave.

Central Ave.

Island Heights

Toms River

River Ave.

# Cattus Island-Island Heights

## Start:

Cattus Island County Park, Toms River, Ocean County. Garden State Parkway to Exit 82. East on Route 37 to Fischer Boulevard. Left on Fischer Boulevard to Cattus Island Boulevard. Follow signs to park entrance. Parking is located adjacent to the Cooper Environmental Center.

## Rides:

**Ride A** is 2.0 miles on a dirt park service road with no traffic.

**Ride B** is 11.9 miles on paved roads with moderate to heavy traffic.

Despite their names, neither of these areas is really an island. However, both are welcome respites from the development that has overtaken this area in the last 30 years. Cattus Island County Park occupies 500 acres of wetlands, beachfront and upland forest jutting between Silver and Barnegat bays. With the passage of the Wetlands Act in 1970 the county acquired the land and developed a small, beautiful park. It's one of the better places to see the transition from the Pine Barrens to coastal wetlands.

Located just a short distance from Cattus Island is Island Heights. The pretty, well-maintained town sits on a low rise, which slopes down toward the Toms River. It dates from the 1870s when it started as a Methodist camp meeting. A small town, with lovely Victorian homes and gardens grew up around the camp meeting ground. Today, as thousands of tourists speed by the town's out-skirts to the hustle and bustle of the shore, this town remains as a reminder of quieter times.

Ride A is a very short ride along the park's service road through wetlands and upland forests out to the edge of Silver Bay. If you want, you can combine this with a hike along some of the park's six miles of hiking trails (no bikes allowed). Information and trail maps are available from the Cooper Environmental Center.

185

Ride B leaves the park through a residential section of Dover Township to Island Heights. It then continues through historic Toms River Village, where there are a number of interesting sites.

Although I have made every effort to eliminate sections of the heavier traffic in the area, this is a fairly crowded area and you will encounter traffic most of the year. Tuesdays and Saturdays are a good time for this tour because both the Ocean County Historical Society and the Toms River Seaport Society Maritime Museum are open. Call (908) 341-1800 and (908) 349-9209 respectively, for more information on these excellent sites.

## Directions: Ride A

**0.0** **Exit parking toward the Cooper Environmental Center. Immediately bear left at bicyclists' sign and turn right on dirt park service road. The center will be on the right as you ride northeast.**

Start your visit at the center. You can pick up some informational brochures and a trail map. Throughout the year, there are a number of very good educational programs about the area's ecology. Call (908) 270-6960 for more information.

The road immediately passes through an open wetlands area. Look across the wetlands and you will see an Osprey platform. Common plant species here are Chairmaker's Rush *(Scirpus americanus)* and Salt Hay *(Juncus gerardi)*. Salt Hay was an important 19th-century agricultural product here and along much of the Jersey Coast. In the summer crews would scythe the rushes, mounding it in large stacks much like regular hay. It was used as cattle feed.

As you continue, you travel through a swamp area that gives way to an upland forest. Besides the dominant Pitch Pines and American Hollies, look for Clammy Azalea (Rhododendron viscosum). It blooms in June and early July. There are almost 300 plant species in the park.

**1.0** **End of road. Return toward parking.**

There is a little beach on the edge of Silver Bay. Cattus Island is called an island because from the bay at high tide, surrounded by water, it appears that way.

**2.0** **Parking. End of tour.**

# Directions: Ride B

**0.0  Exit parking toward park entrance.**

Continue through this mixed pine/oak forest.

**0.6  Stop. Right on Cattus Island Boulevard.**

**0.6  Traffic light. Left on Fischer Boulevard. Use caution.**

**0.7  Right on Hazlewood Road.**

**0.8  Left on Neville street.**

Follow this road as it bends through a residential section.

**1.3  Stop. Left on Bay Avenue.**

**1.3  Traffic light. Right on Coolidge Avenue.**

This two-lane road has a good shoulder as you continue past more houses.

**2.1  Flashing yellow. Continue straight at Windsor Avenue intersection, still on Coolidge Avenue.**

**2.6  Traffic light. Continue straight at Route 37 intersection, still on Coolidge Avenue.**

**2.7  Stop. Continue straight at Morris Boulevard, still on Coolidge Avenue.**

**2.8  Stop. Right on Elizabeth Avenue.**

**3.3  Stop. Left on Central Avenue. Continue downhill to river.**

It's well worth the extra effort to take a short tour through Island Heights along the surrounding side streets. It will only add an additional mile or two to this tour.

There is a country store at 3.7 miles on the left.

**3.8  Intersection of Central Avenue and River Avenue. Right on River Road.**

Alongside scenic Toms River you'll find a pavilion, dock and small riverfront walkway. You couldn't ask for a nicer place to take a ride break. It's easy to lose track of time relaxing by the river. If you look along the river to the houses on the small bluff, you'll discover where the town got its "heights" name.

**4.1  Bear right, still on River Road.**

**4.4  Stop. Bear left, now on West End Road.**

**4.6  Left on Whittier Drive.**

You leave Island Heights and enter Toms River.

**5.3**  **Traffic light. Left on Washington Street.**

Use caution, more traffic the rest of the ride.

**5.9**  **Traffic light. Continue straight at intersection with Clifton Avenue. Follow the side tour directions or skip to the next turn.**

After passing the Toms River Country Club, you enter "downtown" Toms River Village. Many Ocean County and Dover Township office buildings are located in this area.

As with Island Heights, you may want to ride along some side streets before continuing the tour. The following directions are meant as a general guide. First, turn left on Dock Street riding toward the river and bear right on Water Street. The Toms River Seaport Society Maritime Museum is at the intersection of Hooper Avenue and Water Street. They have a great collection of boats and other artifacts relating to Toms River's history as a seaport. Continue along Water Street to Main Street where there is small Huddy Park. It is named for Captain Joshua Huddy, who defended the town's saltworks and blockhouse from a Tory attack in March, 1782. Huddy was later captured and hanged. Return on Main Street to Washington Street. Turn right and continue through traffic light at Hooper Avenue. Before this intersection, on the corner of Allen and Washington streets is the 1850 Courthouse. Resume tour at Hadley Avenue and Washington Street.

**6.7**  **Right on Hadley Avenue. Continue through cross streets.**

The Ocean County Historical Museum is located a few houses in after you turn. This museum has a number of interesting displays and artifacts. Adjoining the museum is an historical and genealogical research facility.

**7.1**  **Bear left on Lafayette/Hadley Avenue.**

**7.2**  **Stop. Right on Route 547/549 (Hooper Avenue).**

**7.4**  **Traffic light. Continue straight at intersection with Terrace Avenue, still on Route 547/549.**

**7.6**  **Traffic light. Continue across Route 37, still on Route 539.**

**7.7**  **Right on Cedar Grove Road. Watch for turning traffic along this road.**

**8.2** Traffic light. Continue straight at Frann Avenue, still on Cedar Grove Road.

**8.5** Bear left, still on Cedar Grove Road.

The rest of the ride goes through a residential section of Dover Township.

**8.9** Traffic light. Right on Bay Avenue.

**10.0** Traffic light. Continue straight at intersection with Vaughn Avenue, still on Bay Avenue.

**10.3** Traffic light. Continue straight across Dunedin Street, still on Bay Avenue.

**10.6** Left on Neville Street.

**11.1** Stop. Right on Hazlewood Road.

**11.2** Stop. Left on Route 37. Use caution crossing and turning on Route 37.

**11.3** Traffic light. Right on Cattus Island Boulevard.

**11.3** Left at park entrance.

**11.9** Parking. End of tour.

The Toms River at Island Heights on a blustery spring day.

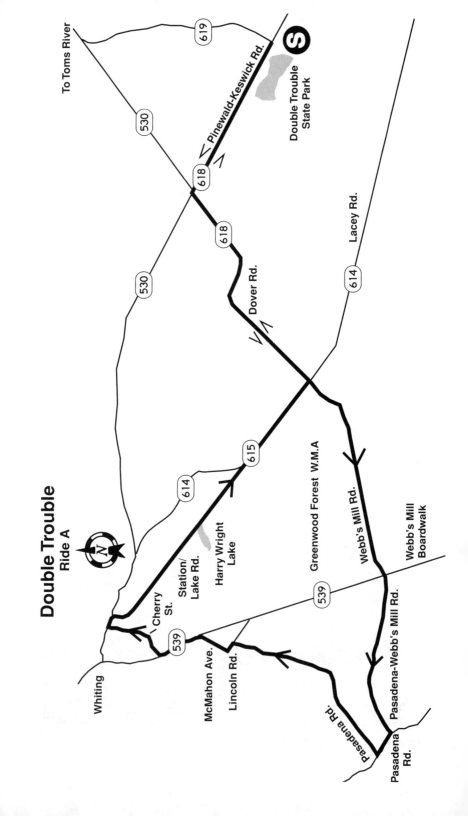

# Double Trouble
## Ride A

To Toms River

619

530

530

618

Pinewald-Keswick Rd.

S

Double Trouble State Park

618

Dover Rd.

Lacey Rd.

614

N

614

615

Station/Lake Rd.

Harry Wright Lake

Greenwood Forest W.M.A

Webb's Mill Rd.

Webb's Mill Boardwalk

Cherry St.

Whiting

539

McMahon Ave.

Lincoln Rd.

539

Pasadena-Webb's Mill Rd.

Pasadena Rd.

Pasadena Rd.

# Double Trouble

## Start:

Double Trouble State Park, Berkeley Township, Ocean County. From Toms River take Route 619 (Double Trouble Road) south to intersection with Route 618 (Pinewald-Keswick Road). Entrance to Double Trouble State Park is across from this intersection. Parking is next to the park entrance.

## Rides:

**Ride A** is 29.2 miles on paved and dirt/sand roads with little to moderate traffic.

**Ride B** is 65.1 miles on paved roads with moderate to heavy traffic.

The Pine Barrens are an important habitat for over 50 amphibians and reptiles. A number of them are endangered in New Jersey and a few are on the federal list of endangered and threatened species. The Pine Barrens Treefrog *(Hyla andersoni)* is probably the best known example. Its habitat is limited to cedar swamps and bogs within the Pine Barrens and is found in only a few other places in the country. Although it is only an inch and a half long, it is a stunningly beautiful creature, with a bright emerald back and lavender sides bordered by a white stripe.

The area of these rides contains important habitat for many amphibian and reptile species. Drained by the Toms River/Cedar Creek watershed, it is an area protected by a state park and five wildlife management areas. However, it is also one of the fastest growing areas in the state, containing two large military facilities at Fort Dix and Lakehurst Naval Air Station. Efforts are currently underway by private and public groups to purchase as much unprotected land as possible before it is lost forever.

These rides also go by some of the more interesting historic sites, small towns and buildings in this area of Ocean County. Ride A goes off-road through Greenwood

Wildlife Management Area to the Webb's Mill Bog Cedar Swamp, where you can take a short hike on a boardwalk through the swamp. The ride continues to Pasadena, returning past Harry Wright Lake on mostly paved roads. Ride B goes through Whiting, continuing through farmland to Cassville, a small town with a Russian restaurant and an imposing gold-domed Russian Church. It returns through Lakehurst, past the huge blimp hangars. Double Trouble is, as yet, an undeveloped state park. Call (908) 341-6662 for more information.

## *Directions: Ride A*

**0.0   Exit park to left on Route 618 (Pinewald-Keswick Road).**

In the 18th century there was a mill near here and cedar was harvested from the surrounding area. Starting in 1909, it became one of the largest cranberry producing centers in the state. Before starting the ride take a walk by some of the old village buildings and along the cranberry bogs. Double Trouble State Park contains over 5,000 acres of surrounding pine forest and cedar swamps.

**2.6   Traffic light. Left on Route 618 (Dover Road).**

A walk-in camping area of the state park is on the left at 3.9 miles and a canoe walk-in area is at 4.2 miles. This is a popular put-in spot for a trip down Cedar Creek.

The "no mowing" signs along the road are there to tell maintenance workers to protect the endangered Pine Barren Gentian *(Gentiana autumnalis)*, which grows right along the road here. If you are riding in September or early October look for a bright blue flower. Environmentalists counted over 800 specimens along the road in 1996.

**6.3   Stop. Continue straight across Route 614 (Lacey Road) intersection, still on Route 618.**

There is a deli at this intersection. The pavement is rough in sections as you continue through the state park. There are a few houses in the Bamber Lake Housing Development.

**7.7   Continue straight as road becomes dirt, now on Webb's Mill Road. Although it is wide, it can be rough.**

This undeveloped area is part of the Greenwood Wildlife Management Area.

**9.4 Bear left, as Cleveland Road (unmarked) comes in on the right, still on Webb's Mill Road.**

This lowland area is drained by Webb's Mill Branch.

**9.8 Stop. Continue straight across Route 539, now on Pasadena-Webb's Mill Road. Stay on this dirt/sand road as it narrows through Greenwood Forest Wildlife Management Area.**

Before continuing, turn left on Route 539 and go 0.1 mile to Greenwood Forest sign on the right. Across from this is an old fence rail. Park your bike here or next to an adjacent tree. Follow the narrow path to the boardwalk and hike the old boardwalk through the swamp. Besides the Pine Barrens Treefrog, look or listen for the Carpenter Frog *(Rana virgatipes)* as you walk along. It gets its name from its call, which resembles a hammer striking a nail twice in a row.

This is also a good place to look for insectivorous plants, including the Round-leaved Sundew *(Drosera rotundifolia)*. It has small pinkish flowers on a long stem above a series of round leaves.

Zebulon Webb built a sawmill alongside the nearby stream in 1774. It and the surrounding small village existed until 1839.

**12.2 Right on Pasadena Road (unmarked), "T" intersection.**

**12.6 Right on Pasadena Road (paved). Follow paved road as it bends north out of wildlife management area.**

Railroad tracks are to the left at this intersection. This was the former location of Pasadena, which was the site of a terra cotta manufacturing plant and clay mine in the late 19th century. Lebanon State Forest is just across the tracks.

**15.8 Bear sharply to the left at Lincoln Road intersection, then bear sharply to the right on McMahon Avenue.**

**16.2 Stop. Left on Route 539 (unmarked).**

Cross out-of-service railroad tracks at 16.6 miles as you ride on the outskirts of Roosevelt City.

**17.0 Right on Cherry Street.**

There is a shopping center to the right at 17.9 miles.

**18.0 Stop. Right on Route 530.**

**18.1 Traffic light. Continue straight at Manchester Boulevard**

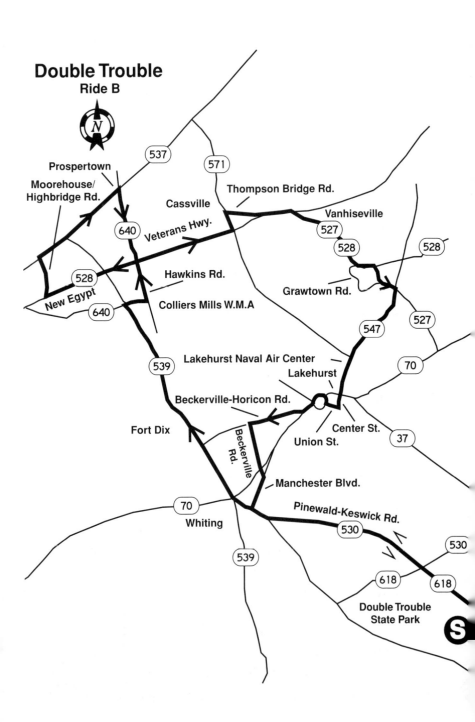

intersection, still on Route 530.

**18.2 Right on Route 615 (Station/Lake Road). Sign for Harry Wright Lake.**

Harry Wright Lake is on the right at 20.2 miles. The benches near the lake area are a good place for a breather. If you want to join the other swimmers, you have to purchase a badge. Across from the lake is a small cedar swamp.

**20.4 Leave park to the right, continuing on Route 615. Road turns to dirt at 20.4 miles.**

**21.4 Stop. Right (straight) on Route 614 (Lacey Road).**

This road goes between the Greenwood Wildlife Management Area on the right and Double Trouble State Park on the left.

The entrance to the Popcorn Park Zoo is on the left at 22.1 miles. This seven-acre zoo provides a haven for abandoned and injured animals. There is a small admission fee that goes to the local humane society. Call (609) 693-1900 for more information.

**22.9 Left on Route 618 (Dover Road).**

There is a deli at this intersection. Continue through the state park as you return to park entrance.

**26.6 Traffic light. Right on Route 618 (Pinewald-Keswick Road).**

**29.2 Park entrance on right. End of tour.**

## Directions: Ride B

**0.0 Exit park to left on Route 618 (Pinewald-Keswick Road).**

**2.6 Traffic light. Continue straight at Route 530/618 intersection, now on Route 530 (Pinewald-Keswick Road). Continue through series of traffic lights after riding through rural area and entering development around Whiting.**

This road has some small hills past the Ocean County Airpark at 4.0 miles. Threatened with development, the land north of here is part of a parcel of land that is being acquired by the Nature Conservancy and New Jersey Natural Land Trust. Part of it will be added to Double Trouble State Park. This is an important habitat area for the Corn Snake (*Elaphe guttata*) and Northern Pine Snake

*(Pituophis melanoleucus),* classified as endangered and threatened, respectively.

**9.4 Traffic light. Continue straight at intersection with Manchester Boulevard, still on Route 530.**

**10.2 Yield right onto Route 539 (Whiting-New Egypt Road).**

**10.4 Traffic light. Continue straight across Route 70 intersection, still on Route 539. Use caution—high speed traffic. There is a good shoulder along most of the road.**

There is an Atlantic White Cedar swamp at 11.6 miles along both sides of Hurricane Branch. Manchester Wildlife Management Area runs on the right along this road. You then ride between Fort Dix on the left and Lakehurst Naval Air Station on the right.

Watch for traffic at the military crossing at 16.3 miles and the National Guard entrance at 16.6 miles.

At 17.3 miles, after you leave the military reservation, there are some houses and a small orchard.

**18.6 Right on Route 640 (Colliers Mills Road).**

There are some small farms along this edge of the Pine Barrens.

**19.5 Stop. Left on Route 640 (Hawkins Road).**

If you want to take a break, continue straight across Route 640 on dirt road into Colliers Mills Wildlife Management Area. It's relaxing to rest alongside the lake. As you continue, you will notice most of the woods are oak rather than Pitch Pine.

**21.1 Flashing red light. Left on Route 528 (Veterans Highway). To shorten the ride by 10.8 miles turn right here and follow the ride directions from 35.7 miles to the finish.**

This crossroads once was a small village known as Archers Corner.

**22.4 Continue straight at Route 539 intersection, still on Route 528.**

**24.7 Right on Moorehouse/Highbridge Road. Continue straight at intersection with Main Street on left.**

If you want to enter New Egypt, continue past this intersection a short distance. There are some small stores and delis in town.

**26.5 Stop. Right on Route 537 (Monmouth-County Line**

Road). Use caution, there is high speed traffic.

**27.4 Continue straight at Route 539 intersection, still on Route 537.**

**29.1 Right on Route 640 (Prospertown Road).**

There are a few old houses in Prospertown. As you continue down this road, you'll ride by one of the many new housing developments being built in the area.

**31.9 Flashing red light. Left on Route 528 (Veterans Highway).**

There is a large oak woods and a swampy area along this road.

**35.7 Traffic light. Left on Route 571 (Cassville Road).**

A couple of delis are at this intersection.

Although historians are unsure, Cassville is a leading candidate for the place where cultivated cranberries were first grown in the Pine Barrens. In the 1840s, John "Peg Leg" Webb transferred wild cranberry vines to a bog here and started domestic cultivation.[23]

**36.2 Right on Thompson Bridge Road.**

Before turning, you will have already seen the gleaming dome of St. Vladimir's Memorial Church. Built in 1940, this is one of the most interesting buildings anywhere in the South Jersey countryside. The church facade has beautiful mosaics. Just past the church on the right is a small garden and a bust of Alexander Pushkin, the famed Russian poet.

Next to the church and parking area are Rova Lake and the Rova Farm Restaurant. The restaurant is open Saturdays, Sundays and Tuesdays and features Russian-American cuisine. Call (908) 928-0928 for more information.

**37.3 Stop. Left on Route 528 (Vanhiseville Road).**

**38.7 Traffic light. Right on Route 527/528 (Vanhiseville-Lakewood Road).**

There is a convenience store at this intersection. The Holmansville Cemetery is on the right at 40.3 miles and then a state forest education center is at 40.6 miles.

**41.6 Bear left at intersection with Grawtown Road, now on Route 528.**

You'll notice more pines as you continue south.

**42.5 Right on Route 527 (Whitesville Road).**

A canoe rental shop on the right at 43.6 miles, offers tours on the nearby Toms River.

**43.9 Traffic light. Right on Route 547 (Chapel-Lakehurst Road).**

Cross railroad tracks at 45.2 miles.

**46.5 Traffic light. Continue straight at intersection with Route 571, still on Route 547.**

At 47.3 miles the huge Lakehurst Hangars are visible. Lakehurst is best known as the site of the *Hindenburg* disaster, which occurred at 7:25 P.M. on May 6, 1937. As the 800-foot-long zeppelin burst into flames, WLS radio announcer Herb Morrison recorded the tragedy with the immortal words, "...this is one of the worst catastrophes in the world! It's a terrific sight. Oh, the humanity..."

To tour the site you must be part of a group tour, which are usually accommodated on Wednesdays. Call (908) 323-2620 for more information.

**47.4 Traffic light. Continue straight at Naval Center entrance, still on Route 547.**

**48.3 Traffic light. Continue straight across Route 70, now on Center Street.**

(If you turn right on Route 70, continue through traffic light at Orchard Street and ride halfway around circle continuing on Route 70. This way, you will not have to ride as far around the following traffic circle, which can be difficult.)

The Lakehurst Museum is located at 300 Center Street. This small, but display-packed building has items relating to local history as well as the heyday of the airship. It is open Wednesdays and Sundays from Noon–3 P.M.. Call (908) 657-8864 for more information.

**48.5 Stop. Right on Union Street.**

There is a good pizza place just to the left at this intersection. As you continue through Lakehurst, scenic Horicon Lake Park is on the left at 48.9 miles, a nice place to break before finishing the rest of the ride.

**49.1 Traffic Circle. Use caution, ride three quarters of the way around the circle on Route 70 west.**

There is a wide shoulder as you leave town.

**50.0 Right on Beckerville-Horicon Road.**

**51.9 Left on Beckerville Road.**

This road goes through Pitch Pines along the edge of the Manchester Wildlife Management Area.

**53.9 Traffic light. Continue straight across Route 70 and immediately bear right on Manchester Boulevard.**

Go briefly through Whiting Wildlife Management Area before entering area of development.

**54.6 Traffic light. Continue straight at intersection with Pleasant Valley Road, still on Manchester Boulevard.**

**55.5 Traffic light. Left on Route 530 (sign for Toms River). Continue through a series of traffic lights on Route 530 as you retrace the route back to Double Trouble State Park.**

**62.5 Traffic light. Continue straight at Route 530 (Dover Road) intersection, now on Route 618 (Pinewald-Keswick Road).**

**65.1 Park entrance on right. End of tour.**

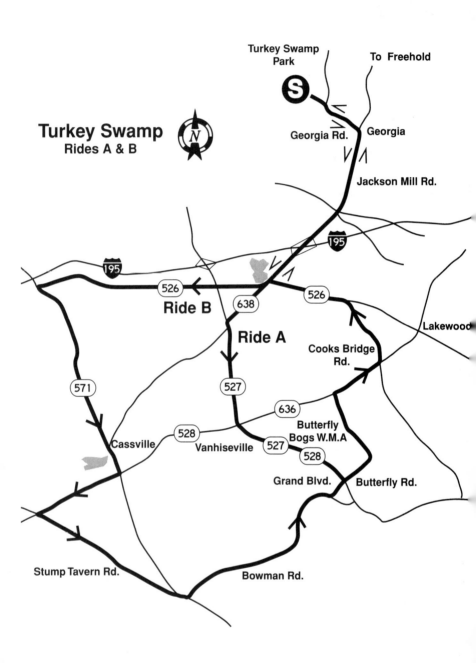

Turkey Swamp Park

To Freehold

**S**

Georgia Rd.

Georgia

Jackson Mill Rd.

# Turkey Swamp
### Rides A & B

195

195

526

526

**Ride B**

638

Lakewood

**Ride A**

Cooks Bridge
Rd.

571

527

636

528

Vanhiseville

527

Butterfly
Bogs W.M.A

528

Cassville

Grand Blvd.

Butterfly Rd.

Stump Tavern Rd.

Bowman Rd.

# Turkey Swamp

## Start:

Turkey Swamp County Park, Monmouth County I-195 to Exit 22. North on Jackson Mill Road. Left on Georgia Road (sign for Turkey Swamp Park). Left at dirt road to parking adjacent to picnic shelter.

## Rides:

**Ride A** is 20.7 miles on paved roads with moderate traffic.

**Ride B** is 32.5 miles on paved roads with moderate traffic. The rides have common starting and ending sections, including a short distance of dirt park road.

Although the Pine Barrens once extended 15 miles into southern Monmouth County, most of this habitat has been altered by development and agriculture. No section of Monmouth County was included in either the New Jersey Pinelands Protection Area or the Federal Pinelands Protection Act. However, there are still some pockets of pinelands fringe habitat, most noticeably at Allaire State Park and Turkey Swamp County Park and adjacent Turkey Swamp Wildlife Management Area.

Turkey Swamp County Park contains about 500 acres of mixed hardwood and pine forest surrounding a 17 acre lake. There are about four miles of hiking trails (no bikes), including one that goes through a small sphagnum bog. Additional facilities include boat rentals, an archery range, picnic areas and campgrounds. If you want to camp here for a weekend and use the park as your home base to tour the surrounding countryside, call (908) 462-7286 for more information or to make reservations.

These rides leave southern Monmouth County going through Jackson Township in northern Ocean County. Only a few decades ago, this was an almost exclusively rural area of small towns, farms and Pine Barrens. Today, although it is still fairly rural, it is a good place to see firsthand the impact of development on the Pine Barrens as more and more farms and woods are replaced by houses and strip malls. These rides overlap some sections of the Double Trouble section, Ride B, through Cassville and Vanhiseville.

## *Directions: Ride A*

**0.0  Exit parking toward Georgia Road on dirt park road.**

The lake is on the right as you leave the park.

**0.3  Stop. Right on Georgia Road (paved).**

Continue through mixed pine/oak woods.

**1.2  Stop. Right on Jackson Mill Road (called Jackson Mills-Freehold Road in Ocean County).**

This small crossroads is called Georgia. The Georgia one-room schoolhouse (now a church) is at this intersection. You leave Monmouth County and enter Ocean County as you ride south. At 2.9 miles there is a pizza place on the left as you continue through the multi- road intersection.

**3.7  Use caution crossing overpass at I-195 intersection. Watch for merging and exiting traffic.**

**4.9  Continue straight at Route 526 intersection, still on Jackson Mill Road.**

At this intersection is Jackson Mills Lake and a restaurant. A sawmill was the main business in the 19th century as it was in many towns that existed at area crossroads.

**5.9  Stop. Left on Route 527 (Cedar Swamp Road).**

There is moderate high speed traffic and a narrow shoulder along this road.

**7.8  Traffic light. Continue straight at intersection with Route 528/636, now on Route 527/528 (Vanhiseville-Lakewood Road).**

This small crossroads was once known as Irish Mills. Its present namc is Vanhiseville, although there is only a convenience store here. The Van Hise family settled in the area before 1675.

The New Jersey State Forestry Resource Center is on the right at 9.4 miles.

**10.0  Left on Butterfly Road (sign for Freehold).**

There are some scenic old cranberry bogs as you ride past the Butterfly Bogs Wildlife Management Area and a campground.

**12.0 Stop. Right on Route 636 (Bennetts Mills Road)**

There is more development as you ride toward Bennetts Mills and the outskirts of Lakewood. The Bennett (Benit) family also settled in the area before 1675.

**13.0 Left on Cooks Bridge Road.**

A strip mall with some convenience stores is at this intersection.

**14.4 Stop. Left on Route 526 (County Line Road).**

**15.8 Stop. Right on Route 638 (Jackson Mills Road).**

Continue over I-195 as you retrace the route back to Turkey Swamp Road.

**19.5 Left on Georgia Road (sign for Turkey Swamp Park).**

**20.4 Left on dirt park road at entrance to park.**

**20.7 Parking adjacent to picnic shelter. End of tour.**

## *Directions: Ride B*

Follow directions for Ride A to 4.9 miles. Instead of going straight turn right on Route 526. This road is rough in spots, bordered mostly by Pitch Pine forest on both sides.

**5.8  Traffic light. Continue straight at Route 527, still on Route 526.**

There continue to be rough spots. Watch for them and also gravel and sand on the edge of the road.

There is increasing development along this road, which is a short distance from I-195 and an easy commute to North Jersey. Jackson Township was incorporated in 1844. With 100.4 square miles, it is the third largest municipality in the state. At the intersection with Burke Road, you go through what was once the small town of Maryland.

**9.1  Stop. Left on Route 571 (Cassville Road).**

**10.5 Bear sharply to the right, then left continuing on Route 571.**

Although there are only a few houses now, the thriving village of Francis Mills was located near the stream crossing, which is one of the little branches of Toms River.

St. Mary's Russian Orthodox Church and cemetery is on the right on the edge of Cassville. You will pass a small park and garden on the right at intersection of Perrineville Road. Look for the bust of Alexander Pushkin. Further along at 12.3 miles is St. Vladimir's Church and Rova Farm Restaurant (see Double Trouble section for more information on this site.)

There are a few delis near the next intersection, after you ride past Rova Lake.

**12.9 Traffic light. Right on Route 528 (Veterans Memorial Highway).**

**14.7 Left on Stump Tavern Road.**

Reportedly Stump Tavern and Hotel was a popular social center in the 19th century. Colliers Mills Wildlife Management Area is on the right side of this road (see the Double Trouble section for more information).

**17.7 Bear right, then stop. Bear right on Route 571 (Cassville Road).**

A convenience store is located just before this intersection.

**17.8 Left on Bowman road. (Sign for Patriot Sports Complex).**

You ride past some houses, a small mobile home park and the sports complex along this road.

**21.4 Left on Grand Boulevard.**

**21.8 Stop. Continue straight at intersection with Route 527/528, now on Butterfly Road.**

At this point follow directions from Ride A at 10.0 miles.

**32.5 Parking adjacent to picnic shelter. End of tour.**

The gold-domed St. Vladimirs Memorial Church dominates the landscape around Cassville.

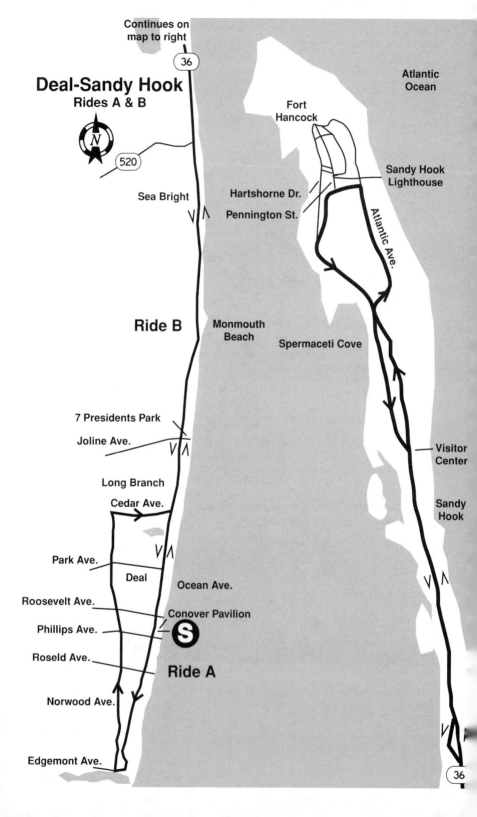

Continues on map to right

36

# Deal-Sandy Hook
### Rides A & B

*N*

520

Atlantic Ocean

Fort Hancock

Sandy Hook Lighthouse

Sea Bright

Hartshorne Dr.

Pennington St.

Atlantic Ave.

## Ride B

Monmouth Beach

Spermaceti Cove

7 Presidents Park

Joline Ave.

Visitor Center

Long Branch

Cedar Ave.

Sandy Hook

Park Ave.

Deal

Ocean Ave.

Roosevelt Ave.

Conover Pavilion

Phillips Ave.

**S**

Roseld Ave.

## Ride A

Norwood Ave.

Edgemont Ave.

36

# Deal-Sandy Hook

## Start:

Conover Pavilion (also known as the Phillips Avenue Pavilion), Deal, Monmouth County. Garden State Parkway to Exit 102. Route 66 east to Asbury Park. North on Route 71, becomes Norwood Avenue in Deal. Right on Phillips Avenue to Ocean Avenue. The pavilion is located adjacent to the beach across from this intersection.

## Rides:

**Ride A** is 7.8 miles on paved roads with moderate to heavy traffic.

**Ride B** is 29.5 miles on paved roads with moderate to heavy traffic.

Gateway National Recreation Area was created by Congress in 1972 to reclaim and preserve some of the important cultural and natural areas around New York Bay. Containing over 27,000 acres, the different units are some of the most visited sites in the national park system, with over six million combined visits in 1995. One of the most popular sections is the Sandy Hook Unit, which is a 6.5-mile-long, 1655-acre barrier peninsula that forms the northernmost part of the Jersey Shore.

Sandy Hook has miles of Atlantic beaches, bay wetlands, and the Fort Hancock historic site, which occupies the northern half of the peninsula. Fort Hancock, established in 1895, was the largest of the series of fortifications to occupy this strategic spot. In 1945, there were 18,000 members of the military stationed here, when it was the headquarters for all New York defenses. The fort was deactivated in 1974 and transferred to the National Park Service.

Parking at Conover Pavilion is free, but if it's summer, get there early for a spot. Beach admission is $4.00. I like this beach because it's more family oriented and less crowded than many of the surrounding beaches. Ride A is a simple loop tour past the large beach estates in Deal and Allenhurst, returning past Monmouth College. Ride B goes north to Sandy Hook through Long Branch, Monmouth Beach and Sea Girt. Ocean Avenue (Route 36) can be very busy most of the year. If you want to eliminate the section of heaviest traffic for Ride B, you can park at Seven Presidents Park at Joline Avenue in Long Branch and follow the ride directions from that point.

## *Directions: Ride A*

**0.0  Exit Conover Pavilion parking to left (south) on Ocean Avenue.**

This stretch of Ocean Drive has some of the most stunning homes on the Jersey Shore. Architectural styles vary from recent designs by leading New York architects to Georgian mansions and Mission-style homes that were built in the 1890s and 1920s.

**0.6  Traffic light. Continue straight at Roseld Avenue, still on Ocean Avenue.**

After you enter Allenhurst, Ocean Drive bears left, then right, as it narrows.

**1.5  Stop. Right on Edgemont Avenue.**

Deal Lake is to your right and beyond that is Asbury Park.

**1.6  Stop. Right on Norwood Avenue (Joins Route 71).**

The Allenhurst Borough Hall is on the right as you return north.

**2.5  Continue straight at intersection with Roseld Avenue, still on Norwood Avenue.**

**2.9  Traffic light. Continue straight at Brighton Avenue, still on Norwood Avenue.**

Watch for parked cars and more traffic as you ride through the small business district.

**3.4  Continue straight at intersection with Roosevelt Avenue, still on Norwood Avenue. Use caution over bridge at railroad tracks.**

Enter into Long Branch, where there are more large estates.

**4.2  Traffic light. Continue straight at intersection with Park Avenue, still on Norwood Avenue.**

There are some interesting buidings on the Monmouth

College Campus. On the left, behind the large ornate fence is the Guggenheim Memorial Library, once the Guggenheim mansion. The campus also contains the Woodrow Wilson Hall, a 130-room mansion that once served as the summer White House.

**4.9  Traffic light. Right on Cedar Avenue. Use caution, four-lane and fairly busy.**

Cross railroad tracks at 5.5 miles.

**5.8  Traffic light. Right on Ocean Avenue.**

**7.0  Traffic light. Continue straight at Lincoln Avenue, still on Ocean Avenue.**

**7.5  Traffic light. Continue straight at intersection with Roosevelt Avenue, still on Ocean Avenue.**

**7.8  Conover Pavilion on left. End of tour.**

## Directions: Ride B

**0.0  Exit Conover Pavilion parking to right (north) on Ocean Avenue. Continue through traffic lights in Deal and enter Long Branch.**

Lake Takanassee and St. Michaels Church are on the left.

**2.0  Traffic light. Continue straight at Cedar Avenue, still on Ocean Avenue. Continue through series of traffic lights through Long Branch. Use special caution for the first few miles, watching for turning traffic. The road goes to three lanes each way, then to two lanes.**

Long Branch was one of America's premier seashore resorts in the 19th and early 20th centuries. It boasted the summer homes of Presidents Grant, Hayes, Garfield, Arthur, Harrison, McKinley and Wilson.

Seven Presidents Park is on the right at 4.1 miles, at the intersection with Joline Avenue. This 33-acre oceanfront park is a good place for a ride break.

**5.4  Traffic light. Continue straight at intersection with Beach Avenue, still on Ocean Avenue, now called Route 36.**

As you continue through Monmouth Beach there are some stores and restaurants.

**7.3  Traffic light. Bear slightly left through Center Street intersection, still on Route 36. Continue through**

**subsequent traffic lights at River Street and Route 520.**

There are more stores and restaurants along Route 36 in Sea Bright.

On the right is a newly-completed seawall splashpad. This was constructed to prevent erosion of the seawall base, but will also serve as a path for cyclists and in-line skaters. You can ride along this for the next few miles, although you might find it sandy.

**9.7 Bear right at sign for Sandy Hook. Continue on overpass into park. At park entrance bear right past entrance toll booths. Cyclists do not need to pay an admission fee. Be alert for other cyclists, cars and pedestrians throughout the park.**

The Spermaceti Cove Visitor Center is on the right at 12.0 miles. Do yourself a favor and stop here before continuing your ride. The center, which is a former life saving station, has a bookstore and displays related to the area's ecology. Pick up a map of Fort Hancock so you can do some exploring in a few miles.

As you pass the ranger station you will notice a large stand of American Holly. There are specimens over 100 years old in this grove.

**13.5 Bear right on Atlantic Avenue (sign for North Beach/ Gunnison Beach).**

Just before this next turn is the entrance to Gunnison Beach. The beach is open for swimming daily from Memorial Day through Labor Day. As the road curves to the left, Battery Gunnison, a remnant of the World War II defenses, is on the right.

**14.8 Bear left and then keep straight at North Beach Sign to right.**

Area "G" parking will be on your left after this intersection. The buildings on the left after the parking area are the Marine Academy of Science and Technology. This high school campus is housed in World War II-era buildings.

**15.1 Stop. Left on Pennington Street (unmarked).**

If you want to tour the Fort Hancock area, turn right here and continue through the park. In a short distance you will see the Sandy Hook Lighthouse, which was built in 1764. If you bear left before the lighthouse, the Fort Hancock Museum will be on your right in a short distance. Continue until intersection with Hartshorne Drive, turn left and ride by "Officer's Row" along the bay.

**15.3 Bear left on Hartshorne Drive.**

The Nike Missile Monument at this intersection is a memorial to ten soldiers and civilians killed during testing of the last weapon system in place at the fort. Sandy Hook Bay is to your right as you head south.

**19.7 Bear right as you leave the park (sign for Sea Bright).**

**19.9 Stop. Right on Route 36 south. Continue through series of traffic lights as you retrace the route south.**

Seven Presidents Park is on the left at 25.4 miles.

**27.5 Traffic light. Continue straight at intersection with Cedar Avenue. Continue through traffic lights as you reenter Deal.**

**29.5 Conover Pavilion on left. End of tour.**

**Officers' Row at Fort Hancock.**

# Associations, Clubs and Agencies

Remember that addresses and telephone numbers change. The Department of Transportation Bicycle Advocate periodically updates a listing of these associations and clubs. This list is available by contacting their office at the address listed below.

## Associations

### Regional

**Bicycle Coalition of the Delaware Valley**, P.O. Box 8194, Philadelphia, PA 19101, (215)-Bicycle

**Bicycle Coalition of NJ Cyclists**, 7584 Remington Ave., Pennsauken, NJ 08110, (609) 488-5843

**BIKE, Inc.**, P.O. Box 667, Chatham, NJ 07928, (201) 635-2211

**Coalition of NJ Cyclists, Inc.**, 66 Witherspoon St., Suite 348, Princeton, NJ 08542, (908) 355-4965

**Forked River Mountain Alliance**, P.O. Box 219, Forked River, NJ 08731

**New Jersey RailTrails**, P.O. Box 23, Pluckemin, NJ 07978, (908) 249-3669

**New Jersey State BMX Association**, c/o Linda Luden, 317 Silzer St., Perth Amboy, NJ 08861, (908) 826-6794

**Pinelands Preservation Alliance**, 114 Hanover St., Pemberton, NJ 08068

**U.S. Bicycling Hall of Fame**, 166 Main St., Somerville, NJ 08876, 1-(800)-Bicycle

**The Whitesbog Preservation Trust**, 120-24A Whitesbog Rd., Browns Mills, NJ 08015, (609) 893-4646

### National

**Adventure Cycling Association** , 150 E. Pine Street, P.O. Box 8308, Missoula,  MT 59807-8303, 1-(800)-721-8719

**Bicycle Federation of America**, 1506 21st St. NW, Suite 200, Washington, DC 20036

**International Mountain Bicycling Association**, P.O. Box 7578, Boulder, CO 80306, (303) 545-9011

**League of American Bicyclists**, 190 W. Ostend St., Suite 120, Baltimore, MD 21230-9850, 1-(800)-288-Bike

**National Off-Road Bicycle Association**, 1750 E. Boulder St., Colorado Springs, CO 80909, (719) 578-4717

**Rails to Trails Conservancy**, 1400 Sixteenth St. NW, Washington, DC 20036, (202) 797-5400

**United States Cycling Federation**, 1750 E. Boulder St., Colorado Springs, CO 80909, (719) 578-4581

## *Clubs*

**Atlantic Bicycle Club**, c/o Tom's Atlantic Cyclery, P.O. Box 330, Allenwood, NJ 08720

**Central Jersey Bicycle Club**, P.O Box 2202, Edison, NJ 08818

**Century Road Club of America**, c/o Kopps Bicycle Shop, 38 Spring St., Princeton, NJ 08542

**East Coast Bicycle Club of Ocean County, Inc.**, c/o Pat Cividanes, 44 Edith Ct., Toms River, NJ 08753

**Egg Harbor Township BMX**, c/o Les Vanderhoff, Veterans Memorial Park, Ocean Heights Ave., Bargaintown, NJ 08232

**Family Cycling** , c/o Barbara and Mel Kornbluh, RR #8, P.O Box 319E, Gwynwood Drive, Bridgeton, NJ 08318

**Jersey Shore Touring Society**, P.O Box 8581, Red Bank, NJ 07701

**Morris Velo Sports Club**, c/o Sarah Frost, 5 Rose Lane, Summit, NJ 07901

**Mullica Hill BMX Racing**, 405 Megan Drive, Mickletown, NJ 08056

**Outdoor Club of South Jersey, Inc.**, 209 Lindsay Ave., Runnemede, NJ 08078-1742

**PMK Cycling, Inc.**, c/o Robin Snyder Bauer, 44 Broadway, Freehold, NJ 07728

**Princeton Free Wheelers**, P.O. Box 1204, Princeton, NJ 08542-1204

**Shore Cycling Club**, c/0 Dianne Silverstein, 16 Laurel Ave., Linwood, NJ 08221

**Sierra Club, New Jersey State Chapter**, 57 Mountain Ave., Princeton, NJ 08540

**Sierra Club, West Jersey Group**, 9 Randolph Dr., Mt. Holly, NJ 08060-1142

**South Jersey Wheelmen**, c/o Terry Ladue, P.O. Box 2705, Vineland, NJ 08360

**Summit Cycling Club**, c/o Tom Simpson, 437 Summer Ave., Beverly, NJ 08010

**Wheelmen**, c/o Tom W. Green, 394 Griscom Dr., Salem, NJ 08079

**Wrecking Crew**, c/o Rick Rosseter, 2905 Taft St., Wall, NJ 07719

## Agencies

### State Parks, Forests and Historic Sites

**Allaire State Park**, P.O. Box 220, Farmingdale, NJ 07727, (908)938-2371

**Barnegat Lighthouse State Park**, P.O. Box 167, Barnegat Light, NJ 08006, (609) 494-2016

**Bass River State Forest**, P.O. Box 118, New Gretna, NJ 08224, (609) 296-1114

**Belleplaine State Forest**, Route 550, Woodbine, NJ 08270, (609) 861-2404

**Cape May Point State Park**, Box 107, Cape May Point, NJ 08212, (609) 884-2159

**Corson's Inlet State Park**, Ocean Drive , Ocean City, NJ 08226, (609) 861-2404

**Double Trouble State Park**, P.O. Box 175, Double Trouble and Pinewald Keswick Rds., Bayville, NJ 08721, (908) 341-6662

**Fort Mott State Park**, RD 3, Box 543, Salem, NJ 08079, (609) 935-3218

**Hancock House**, P.O. Box 139, Hancocks Bridge, NJ 08038, (609) 935-4373

**Island Beach State Park**, Seaside Park, NJ 08752, (908) 793-0506

**Lebanon State Forest**, P.O. Box 215, New Lisbon, NJ 08064, (609) 726-1191

**Parvin State Park**, RD 1, Box 374, Elmer, NJ 08318, (609) 358-8616

**Penn Sate Forest**, c/o Bass River Forest, P.O. Box 118, New Gretna, NJ 08224, (609) 296-1114

**Twin Lights**, Lighthouse Road, Highlands, NJ 07732, (908) 872-1886

**Wharton State Forest**, Batsto RD #9, Hammonton, NJ 08037, (609) 561-0024

## State Agencies

**New Jersey Department of Environmental Protection, Division of Fish, Game & Wildlife**, 501 East State St., CN 400, Trenton, NJ 08625-0400

**New Jersey Department of Transportation, Bicycle Advocate**, 1035 Parkside Ave., CN 617, Trenton, NJ 08625

**New Jersey Division of Parks and Forestry**, CN 404, Trenton, NJ 08625

**New Jersey Division of Travel and Tourism**, CN 826, Trenton, NJ 08625-0826

**Pinelands Commission**, P.O. Box 7, New Lisbon, NJ 08064

## National Agencies

**Edwin B. Forsythe National Wildlife Refuge**, P.O. Box 72, Rt. 9, Oceanville, NJ 08231, (609) 652-1665

**Gateway National Recreation Area**, Sandy Hook Unit, P.O. Box 530, Fort Hancock, NJ 07732, (908) 872-0115

**National Park Service**, NJ Coastal Heritage Trail, PO Box 118, Mauricetown, NJ 08329

**U.S. Department of the Interior, Geological Survey**, Reston, VA 22092

**U.S. Fish and Wildlife Service**, Delaware Bay Coastal Ecosystems Program , 2610 Whitehall Neck Road, Smyrna, DE 19977

# Bicycle Shops and Rental Stores

This list includes only those businesses located in or near the area covered by this book. There are many other shops located in adjacent counties and states which service this area.

## Cape May, Cumberland and Salem Counties

Algie's Place
114 E. 17th Ave.
Wildwood, NJ 08260
(609) 729-5669

Annarelli's Bicycle Store
1014 Asbury Ave.
Ocean City, NJ 08226
(609) 399-2238

Beacon Cycling & Fitness
1362 S. Delsea Dr.
Vineland, NJ. 08360
(609) 696-2666

Bradley's Bikes
Rambler Rd.
Wildwood Crest, NJ 08260
(609) 729-1444

Crest Bicycles
500 E. Heather Rd.
Wildwood Crest, NJ 08260
(609) 522-5763

Delsea Bike Shop
116 Route 47
Dias Creek, NJ 08210
(609) 465-9420

Ed's Bike Shop
1377 N. Delsea Dr.
Vineland, NJ 08360
(609) 691-5757

Green Acres Bike Shop
Bridgeton-Millville Pike
Bridgeton, NJ 08302
(609) 455-7531

Hale Sports
3-5 Mechanic St.
Cape May Court House,
NJ 08210
(609) 465-3126

Harbor Bike & Beach
9828 3rd Ave.
Stone Harbor, NJ 08247
(609) 368-3691

Hollywood Bicycle Center
2544 Dune Dr.
Avalon, NJ 08202
(609) 967-5846

Hollywood Bicycle Center
4601 Landis Ave.
Sea Isle City, NJ 08243
(609) 263-0232

Kona Bike Shop
Rio Grande & New Jersey Aves.
Wildwood, NJ 08260
(609) 522-7899

Ocean City Bicycle Center
8th & Atlantic Ave.
Ocean City, NJ 08226
(609) 399-5550

Pat's Bicycles
613 8th St.
Ocean City, NJ 08226
(609) 399-5220

S&R Schwinn Sales
100 N. High st.
Millville, NJ 08332
(609) 327-1311

Shields Bike Rentals
11 Gurney Ave.
Cape May, NJ 08204
(609) 898-1818

Steck's Bike Rental
319 Beach Dr.
Cape May, NJ 08204
(609) 884-1188

13th Street Bikes
13th St. & Boardwalk
Ocean City, NJ 08226
(609) 399-7121

34th Street Bikes
34th & West Ave.
Ocean City, NJ 08226
(609) 398-6431

12th Street Bike Rentals
12th & Boardwalk
Ocean City, NJ 08226
(609) 399-2814

Tommy's Bicycles
Allmond & Allvine Rd.
Norma, NJ 08347
(609) 692-9146

Village Bicycle Shop
Victorian Village Plaza
Cape May, NJ 08204
(609) 884-8500

Village Schwinn Shop
606 New Road
Somers Point, NJ 08244
(609) 927-3775

Vince's Bikes
4012 Pleasure Ave.
Sea Isle City, NJ 08243
(609) 263-3186

The Wheel House
2743 Dune Drive
Avalon, NJ 08202
(609) 368-5353

## Atlantic, Burlington, Camden and Gloucester Counties

AAA Bike Shop
5300 Ventnor Ave.
Ventnor, NJ 08406
(609) 487-0808

Action Wheels
640 Route 45
Deptford, NJ 08096
(609) 468-5115

Beacon Cycling & Fitness
231 Tilton Rd.
Northfield, NJ 08225
(609) 641-9531

Bicycle Pro Shop
604 Black Horse Pike
Williamstown, NJ 08094
(609) 875-8809

Bill's Bicycles
7-9 E. Broad St.

Palmyra, NJ 08065
(609) 829-0922

Bike Line
185 Route 70
Medford, NJ 08055
(609) 654-6868

Bike Line
Berlin Circle Plaza
Berlin, NJ 08009
(609) 753-7433

Bike Line
Ellisburg Circle
Cherry Hill, NJ 08002
(609) 795-6200

Bike Line
Cross Keys Commons
Turnersville, NJ 08012
(609) 875-1910

Bike World
1929 Michigan Ave.
Atlantic City, NJ 08401
(609) 345-0077

Burlington County Bicycle
Center
43 Charleston Rd.
Willingboro, NJ 08046
(609) 877-8016

Chip-N-Dale
1240 Monmouth Rd.
Mount Holly, NJ 08060
(609) 261-1981

Danzeisen & Quigley
1720 Route 70
Cherry Hill, NJ 08034
(609) 424-5969

Eastern Sports Specialists
3131 Route 70
Mt. Laurel, NJ 08054
(609) 722-1117

Erlton Bicycle Shop
1011 Route 70
Cherry Hill, NJ 08002
(609) 428-2344

Genie Cyclery
510 Stokes Rd.
Medford, NJ 08055
(609) 953-0200

Center Square Shopping
Center
Washington Twp.,NJ 08012
(609) 582-0800

Margate Bike Shop
19 Essex Ave.
Margate, NJ 08402
(609) 822-9145

Mini Trail Bikes
307 N. White Horse Pike
Lindenwold, NJ 08021
(609) 783-5932

Mount Holly Bicycle Shop
1613 Route 38
Mt. Holly, NJ 08060
(609) 267-6620

Peddler's Shop
Route 41 S.
Deptford, NJ 08096
(609) 228-7800

The Peddler's Shop
70 E. Main St.
Marlton, NJ 07746
(609) 983-4333

Pitman Bike World
425 S. Broadway
Pitman, NJ 08071
(609) 582-0626

Pro Pedals
684 S. White Horse Pike
Hammonton, NJ 08037
(609) 561-3030

Ricco's Cyclery
600 S. Route 30
Somerdale, NJ 08083
(609) 783-3035

Workman's
79 E. Main St.
Moorestown, NJ 08057
(609) 234-6286

## Ocean and Monmouth Counties

A-1 Bicycles
642 Arnold Ave.
Pt. Pleasant, NJ 08742
(908) 295-2299

AJ's Rentals
311 S. Bay Ave.
Beach Haven, NJ 08008
(609) 492-2626

Allenhurst Cycle Shop
316 Main St.
Allenhurst, NJ 07711
(908) 517-0777

Atlantic Cyclery
188 First Ave.
Atlantic Highlands, NJ 07716
(908) 291-2664

Beachwood Bicycles
101 Route 166
Beachwood, NJ 08722
(908) 349-2333

Beacon Cycling & Fitness
575 Fischer Blvd.
Toms River, NJ 08753
(908) 929-2999

The Bicycle Hub
455 Route 520
Marlboro, NJ 07746
(908) 972-8822

Bicycle World
2449 Route 9 N.
Howell, NJ 07731
(908) 431-5610

Bicycles Unlimited
67 E. County Line Rd.
Lakewood, NJ 08701
(908) 363-2453

Brielle Cyclery
205 Union Ave.
Brielle, NJ 08730
(908) 528-9121

Brigg's Bicycles
8401 Long Beach Blvd.
Beach Haven Crest, NJ 08008
(609) 492-1143

Brigg's Bicycles
63 E. Bay Ave.
Manahawkin, NJ 08050
(609) 597-5999

Bud's Bikes
125 New Jersey Ave.
Absecon, NJ 08201
(609) 641-8060

Cag's Cycles
821 Broadway
West Long Branch, NJ 07764
(908) 229-6683

D.J.'s Cycles
15th & Main St.
Belmar, NJ 07719
(908) 681-8228

D.J.'s Cycle & Fitness
94 Brighton Ave.
Long Branch, NJ 07740
(908) 870-2277

Faria's Sales & Rentals
220 Centre St.
Beach Haven, NJ 08008
(609) 492-7484

Freehold Bicycles
85 Village Center Dr.
Freehold Twp., NJ 07728
(908) 431-0266

Fun & Sports
88 Route 9 N.
Marlboro, NJ 07746
(908) 536-0606

Glendola Bicycle
2709 Belmar Blvd.
Wall Twp., NJ 07719
(908) 681-5264

Jerry's Bicycle Shop
1522 Route 37
Toms River, NJ 08753
(908) 929-1155

Jobe's Seashore Rentals
2306 S. Bay Ave.
Beach Haven, NJ 08008
(609) 492-3298

Manasquan Bicycle Center
128 Main St.
Manasquan, NJ 08736
(908) 223-2444

Michael's Bicycle Co.
2857 Route 35
Hazlet, NJ 07730
(908) 739-0333

Mike's Bikes
46 First Ave.
Atlantic Highlands, NJ 07716
(908) 291-8822

Padi's Pedal Power Bicycles
1177 Fischer Blvd.
Toms River, NJ 08753
(908) 270-5920

Pedal Power Bicycle Shop
386 Route 9
Cedar Run, NJ 08092
(609) 597-9388

The Peddler
1500 Ocean Blvd.
Long Branch, NJ 07740
(908) 229-6623

The Peddler
21 White Ave.
Red Bank, NJ 07701
(908) 219-6666

Point Pleasant Bicycles
2701 Bridge Ave.
Point Pleasant, NJ 08742
(908) 899-9755

Precision Cycles
197 Wall Rd.
West Long Branch, NJ 07764
(908) 222-9255

Rossi's Rent A Rama
1607 Bay Blvd.
Ortley Beach, NJ 08751
(908) 793-8573

Roy's Barnegat Bicycle Ranch
107 S. Main St.
Barnegat, NJ 08005
(609) 698-6627

Shrewsbury Bicycles
765 Route 35
Shrewsbury, NJ 07702
(908) 741-2799

Tyres Bicycles
1900 Blvd.
Seaside Park, NJ 08752
(908) 830-2050

Walters
418 Long Beach Blvd.
Ship Bottom, NJ 08008
(609) 494-1991

# Calendar of Events

This is a partial listing of biking and other area events. Dates and telephone numbers can change. To get an up-to-date twice yearly "New Jersey Calendar of Events" contact the New Jersey Department of Commerce of Commerce and Economic Development, Division of Travel and Tourism, CN 826, Trenton, NJ 08625; (609) 292-2470.

## April

Cape May, Spring Victorian Weekend, 1-(800)-275-4278

Fort Mott, Earth Day Celebration, (609) 935-3218

Mays Landing, Earth Day Celebration, (609) 343-5089

Ocean County, Earth Day Cleanup, (908) 506-9090

Somers Point, Bayfest, (609) 927-5253

Tabernacle, Carranza Individual Time Trial, (609) 228-7800

Waretown, Spring Pinelands Music Festival, (609) 971-1593

Wharton State Forest, Earth Day Trail Cleanup (609) 576-4559

Wildwood, Project Pride, (609) 729-6818

## May

Batsto, Spring Wildflowers of the Pinelands, (609) 567-4559

Batsto, Pinelands Triple Loop Bike Rides, (908) 652-0880

Cape May/Statewide, Audubon's World Series of Birding, (609) 884-2736

Cold Spring Village, Festival of American Crafts, (609) 898-2300

Delaware Bay Beaches, Shorebird Migration, (609) 292-9400

Egg Harbor City, Renault Winery Spring Hoe-Down Craft Festival, (609) 965-2111

Lincroft, Farmlands Century Bike Tour, (908) 225-HUBS

Long Beach Island, Tour de Ocean Bike-a-Thon, (908) 929-0660

Long Branch, Sunrise Run-Bike-Run, (908) 842-4000

Sandy Hook, MS Coast the Coast Bike Tour, (908) 681-2322

Seaside Park, Annual Arts and Crafts Festival, (908) 914-0100

Smithville, Mayfest, (609) 652-0001

Somerville, Main Street Sprints, (908) 707-0249

Somerville, Tour of Somerville, (908) 725-0461

Villas, Robert Coombs Run, (609) 886-7880

Waretown, Pine Barrens Festival, (609) 971-1593

## *June*

Absecon, Atlantic City Rescue Mission Bike-A-Thon, (609) 965-4823

Batsto, Decoy & Woodcarvers Show, (609) 561-3262

Belmar, New Jersey Seafood Festival, (908) 681-0005

Bridgeton, Dutch Neck Village Strawberry Festival, (609) 451-2188

Bridgeton, Folk Festival, 1-(800)-319-3379

Cape May, Seafood Festival, 9609) 884-5508

Delaware Bayshore Communities, Delaware Bay Day, (609) 785-2060

Fort Mott State Park, Get Ready Metric Century, (609) 848-6123

High Point to Cape May, Longest Day Double Century Bike Ride, (908) 233-9094

Lincroft, Big Sisters/Brothers Bike-A-Thon, (908) 530-9800

Manahawkin, Stafford Township Founders Day, (609) 597-1660

Parvin State Park, Thunder Gust Triathlon, (609) 963-2772

Point Pleasant, Summerfest, (908) 899-7240

Point Pleasant Beach, Coors Light Cycling Classic, (908) 899-9753

Seaside Heights, Seaside Heights Triathlon, (908) 830-7260

Somerville, U.S. Bicycling Hall of Fame Criterium, (908) 722-3620

Statewide, National Trails Day, (609) 984-1339

Statewide, American Diabetes Asociation Tour de Cure, 800-Tour-888

Toms River, State Chili Cook-Off, (908) 240-1001

# July

Barnegat Light, 4th of July Parade, (609) 494-3522

Belmar, Belmar Sand Castle Contest, (908) 681-0005

Bridgeton, 4th of July Celebration, 1-(800)-319-3379

Edison, Garden State Games, (908) 225-0303

Harvey Cedars, Craft Day By the Bay, (609) 494-2843

Long Beach Island, Long Beach Island Arts Festival, (609) 494-5556

Long Branch, Oceanfest, (908) 222-0400

Seaside Park, The Patriotic Bike Parade, (908) 914-0100

Tabernacle, Carranza Memorial Ceremony, (609) 561-0024

Tuckerton, Baymen's Festival, (609) 296-8868

Whitesbog, Whitesbog Blueberry Festival, (609) 893-4646

Williamstown, July 4th Extravaganza, (609) 728-9823

# August

Bridgeton, Bridgeton Zoo Ride, (609) 848-6123

Cold Spring Village, Farmfest, (609) 898-2300

East Point Lighthouse, Artists Day, (609) 825-9662

Fort Mott, Civil War Reenactment, (609) 935-3218

Harvey Cedars, Dog Day Road Race, (609) 361-9364

Long Beach Island, Arts and Crafts Show, (609) 494-1241

Manahawkin, Good Ol' Days, (609) 597-3211

Middletown, Woods Hollow Classic Mountain Bike Race, (908) 842-4000

Salem, Historic Market Street Day, (609) 935-0896

Sea Isle City, 10 Mile Island Run, (609) 263-TOUR

Stone Harbor, Arts & Crafts Festival,(609) 368-5021

Toms River, MS Cycling Classic, 1-(800)-Bicycle

# September

Barnegat, Barnegat Pirates' Day, (609) 698-8967

Brielle, Brielle Day, (908) 528-6600

Cape May, New Jersey Audubon's Annual Cape May Autumn Weekend, (609) 884-2736

Cape May Court House, Holy Redeemer Fall Fun Bike-A-Thon, (609) 465-5000

Cherry Hill to Ocean City, MS 150 City to Shore Bike Tour, (609) 858-6900

Cold Spring Village, 19th-Century Harvest Days, (609) 898-2300

Cold Spring Village, Native-American Celebration, (609) 898-2300

Crosswicks, Crosswicks Village Festival, (609) 298-2311

Egg Harbor City, Renault Winery Grape Stomping Festival, (609) 965-2111

Greenwich, Craft Faire, (609) 451-8454

Island Beach, Island Beach Triathlon, (609) 468-0010

Lakewood, Ocean County Folk Arts Festival, (908) 506-9090

Long Beach Island, International Coastal Cleanup Day, (609) 492-0222

Long Branch, The Sprint Triathlon, (908) 842-4000

Mauricetown, Seafood Festival, (609) 785-1538

Middletown, JSTS Century Ride, (908) 364-8088

Parvin State Park, Jersey Devil Century, (609) 848-6123

Pennsville, Septemberfest, (609) 678-3049

Point Pleasant Beach, Festival of the Sea, (609) 899-2424

Sandy Hook, Shore Heritage Festival, (908) 872-0115

Sea Isle City, Fall Family Festival, (609) 263-TOUR

Seaside Heights, Fall Fest, (908) 793-1510

Toms River, Ride for the Blind, (908) 288-9352

Tuckerton, Old Time Barnegat Bay Decoy & Gunning Show, (609) 971-3085

Waretown, Ocean County Bluegrass Festival, (609) 791-1593

## October

Allaire Village, Crafter's Market, (908) 938-2253

Batsto, Annual Country Living Fair, (609) 561-5019

Bay Head, Harvest Festival, (908) 899-0767

Belleplaine State Forest, Belleplaine Beacon Century Biking Event, (609) 652-0880

Belmar, Fall Festival, (908) 681-0005

Bordentown, Cranberry Festival, (609) 298-0505

Bridgeton, Fall Festival, (609) 451-2188

Cape May, Victorian Week, (609) 884-5404

Chatsworth, Cranberry Festival,(609) 859-9701

Cold Spring Village, Pumpkin Festival, (609) 898-2300

Estell Manor, Great Pumpkin Duathlon (609) 391-8123

Long Beach Island, Chowderfest Weekend, (609) 494-7211

Long Beach Island, 18 Mile Run, (609) 494-8861

Monmouth County, Lenape Weekend,(908) 291-4206

Sandy Hook, War at the Shore Biathlon, (908) 842-4317

Wells Mills, Pine Barrens Jamboree, (609) 971-3085

West Cape May, Lima Bean Festival, (609) 884-4656

Whitesbog, Cranberry Harvest Tour, (609) 893-4646

Wildwood, Heritage Festival, (609) 729-6818

## November

Cape May, The Bird Show, (609) 884-2736

Mauricetown, Craft Show, (609) 785-2861

Ocean City, Quiet Festival, (609) 525-9300

Ocean Grove, Harvest Home Festival, (908) 502-0303

Waretown, Homeplace Reunion Festival, (609) 971-1593

Whitesbog, Fat Tire Bike Tour, (609) 893-4646

Whitesbog, Whitesbog History Tour, (609) 893-4646

## *December*

Batsto, Holiday Tours of Batsto Mansion, (609) 561-3262

Cape May, Christmas Candlelight Tour,(609) 884-5404

Mauricetown, Christmas Candlelight House Tour, (609) 785-1137

Ocean Grove, Victorian Holiday Festival, (908) 502-0303

Salem, Yuletide Tour of Salem City, (609) 935-0896

Whitesbog, Candlelight Tour, (609) 893-4646

# Internet Resources

There is a wealth of information online pertaining to both New Jersey and bicycling. The following is a listing of a few of these sites, a brief description and their addresses.

## Bicycling

**Bicycle Guide.** The online version of the magazine. There are product reviews, ride tips and other general cycling articles. http://www.bicycleguide.com

**Bicycle Coalition of The Delaware Valley**. The homepage of one of the area's largest advocacy groups and riding clubs. Although the club is headquartered in Philadelphia, they sponsor a number of rides in South Jersey. http://www.libertynet.org/~bcdv

**Bicycle Transit Authority**. This site has bicycle repair advice from expert mechanics. If you are interested in buying a new bike there is a list of hundreds of current models and suggested retail price. http://www.bikeinfo.com

**The Global Cycling Network**. Directory of bicycling organizations and a mailing list center to communicate with cyclists from around the world. http://cycling.org

**League of American Bicyclists**: The homepage of one of America's largest bicycling advocacy groups. http://bikeleague.org

**Mid-Atlantic Cycling Pages**. Information about clubs, races and tours in this region. Links to other sites. http://whitman.sprintlink.net

**New Jersey Bicycling**. The bicycling homepage from New Jersey Online. Information on mountain biking and touring in New Jersey. Links to other biking and tourism sites. http://www.nj.com/bike

**NORBA**. The homepage of the National Off Road Bicycling Association. Information about membership and racing. http://www.usacycling.com/norba

**United States Bicycling Hall of Fame.** Information about the organization and its inductees.

http://www.nj.com/bike/hof/top.hof.html

**USCF.** The homepage of the United States Cycling Federation, the governing body of road racing in America. http://www.usacycling.com

**The WWW Bike Lane.** Maintained by Bryn Dole at Purdue University, this page has dozens of links to bicycling sites around the world. http://www.cs.purdue.edu/homes/dole/bike.html

**Yahoo!** Cycling. There are hundreds of links to bicycling sites. http://www.yahoo.com/Recreation/Sports/cycling

## General Information and Tourism

**Atlantic City.** What to do, where to stay and what to see. http://banzai.neosoft.com/citylink/atlantic

**Atlantic County.** General county information. http://commlink.atlantic.county.lib.nj.us

**Camden County.** Information about parks, recreation and area maps. http://www.co.camden.nj.us

**Cape May.** Lots of information about this resort town, including bird watching information and eco-tourism. http://www.covesoft.com/capemay

**Gloucester County**. Information about county resources, including parks and museums. http://www.buyrite.com/gloucester county

**Long Beach Island and Ocean County.** This site has information about real estate, local news, weather and  businesses. Links to history and other sites. http://www.intserv.com/%7Elbi/general.html

**Medford**. Listings for merchants, town events and local attractions. http://medfordnj.com

**New Jersey Online. News**, weather and a variety of links for the Garden State. http://www.nj.com

**The New Jersey Shore**. A good source for information about the entire shore region. Links to other shore sites. Southern and northern shore weather forecasts. http://www.nmark.com/njs

**Pressplus**. The online version of the Press of Atlantic City. News about South Jersey, including the Pine Barrens, Jersey Shore and Delaware Bay Region. http://www.pressplus.com

**Toms River.** Good site for information about Toms River and northern Ocean County. http://www.tomsriverarea.com

**Tuckerton.** Information about the community, annual events and the Barnegat Bay Decoy and Baymen's Museum. http://icsglobal.com/clamtown

## *Historical and Ecological*

**Atlantic White Cedars Project.** Information about this important Pine Barrens tree. http://loki.stockton.edu/~wcedars

**Burlington County Pine Barrens Info**. Very good site for information about the entire region. http://www.burlco.00.burlco.cybernet.net/pinelands

**Cumberland County Nature Study**. A good source of ecological information for the county and Delaware Bay Region. http://www.hsrl.rutgers.edu/http_nature.cc.html

**Georgian College, Plants of the Pine Barrens**. Descriptions and photographs of some of the more well-known plants. http://www.georgian.edu/bi_pines/bi_pb_nj.htm

**Jersey Devil.** One of the best sources of information on the elusive Pine Barrens monster. http://www.intserv.com?shadows/jd.htm

**Jersey Devil**. Another good source for facts about the legend. http://www.netcom.com/%7Ethefix/jdlegend.html

**Maurice River**. History of the shellfishing industry and descriptions of Delaware Bay Region flora and fauna. http://www.igc.apc.org/mauriceriver

**Peterson Online.** Extensive bird watching information, including a calendar of birding events. Operated by Houghton Mifflin, the publisher of the Peterson field guides. http://www.petersononlin.com

**Pinelands Commisssion**. Information about the Pine Barrens and the governmental agency which deals with land use questions in the region. http://www.state.nj.us/pinelands

# Endnotes

1. Also known as the Convention on Wetlands of International importance, the Ramsar Convention took place in Ramsar, Iran in 1971. It was the first modern global treaty on the conservation and use of natural resources. 101 countries have signed the treaty and 872 sites are protected. Their official Internet address is: http://iucn.org/themes/ramsar

2. David Perry, *Bike Cult*, New York: Four Walls Eight Windows, 1995, p. 244

3. Sandra Boodman, *The Washington Post*, January 14, 1997, Health Section, p. 5

4. John T. Cunningham, *New Jersey: America's Main Road*, Garden City, N.Y.: Doubleday & Company, 1976, p. 243

5. Henry Charlton Beck, *More Forgotten Towns of Southern New Jersey*, New Brunswick: Rutgers University Press, 1963, pp. 302-309

6. Cunningham, p. 89

7. Beck, pp. 24-28

8. Howard P. Boyd, *A Field Guide to the Pine Barrens of New Jersey*, Medford, NJ: Plexus Publishing, 1991, p. 4

9. Cunningham, pp. 33-34

10. James F. McGloy and Ray Miller, *The Jersey Devil*, Wallingford, PA: The Middle Atlantic Press, 1976.

11. Boyd, p. 57

12. *Edwin B. Forsythe Wildlife Refuge Pamphlet*, Department of the Interior, 1992.

13. Franklin W. Kemp, *A Nest of Rebel Pirates*, Egg Harbor City, NJ: The Laureate Press, 1966, pp. 22-36

14. Beck, pp. 143-47

15. Henry Charlton Beck, *Forgotten Towns of Southern New Jersey*, New Brunswick: Rutgers University Press, 1961, pp. 167-74

16. Beryl Collins and Emily Russell, editors, *Protecting the New Jersey Pinelands*, New Brunswick: Rutgers University Press, 1988, p. 30

17. John McPhee, *The Pine Barrens*, New York: Farrar Straus & Giroux, 1981, pp. 88-90

18. Beck, *Forgotten Towns of Southern New Jersey*, pp. 35-48

19. Ibid, pp. 105-113

20. Kemp, pp. 43-50

21. John Bailey Lloyd, *Eighteen Miles of History on Long Beach Island*, Harvey Cedars, NJ: Down The Shore Publishing, 1994, pp. 50-51

22. Beck, *Forgotten Towns of Southern New Jersey*, pp. 115-18

23. B. Michalsky, *Whitesbog: An Historical Sketch*, Browns Mills, NJ: Conservation and Environmental Studies Center, 1978, p. 17

# Selected Bibliography

John McPhee's *The Pine Barrens* is not only my favorite book on the Pine Barrens, it is one of my favorite books on any subject. If you haven't read it, you must. Try and find the edition with the photographs by Bill Curtsinger. Although Henry Charlton Beck's writing now appears somewhat stilted and you must take his tales with a grain of salt, his histories of South Jersey towns and the region are indispensable. The Peterson birding guide-books are still the best written and illustrated. Consider carry-ing one with you if you like bird watching.

In addition to the following sources, I relied upon the many brochures, pamphlets and maps published by local, state and federal agencies. The bicycling books listed are just a few of the better history and how-to books to be found.

## The New Jersey Shore, Pine Barrens and Delaware Bay Region

Beck, Henry Charlton, *Forgotten Towns of Southern New Jersey*, New Brunswick: Rutgers University Press, 1961

Beck, Henry Charlton, *More Forgotten Towns of Southern New Jersey*, New Brunswick: Rutgers University Press, 1963

Beck, Henry Charlton, Jersey Genesis: *The Story of the Mullica River*, New Brunswick: Rutgers University Press, 1945

Boyd, Howard P., *A Field Guide to the Pine Barrens of New Jersey*, Medford,NJ: Plexus Publishing, Inc., 1991

Cawley, James and Cawley, Margaret, *Exploring the Little Rivers of New Jersey*, New Brunswick: Rutgers University Press,1961

Collins, Beryl Robichaud and Russell, Emily W.B., editors; *Protecting the New Jersey Pinelands*, New Brunswick: Rutgers University Press, 1988

Collins,Joseph T. and Conant, Roger, *A Field Guide to Reptiles and Amphibians*, New York: Houghton Mifflin, 1991

Cunningham, John T., *New Jersey: America's Main Road*, Garden City, NY: Doubleday & Company, 1976

Ewing, S.W.R., *An Introduction to Batsto*, Batsto, NJ: Batsto Citizens Committee 1986

Ewing, S.W.R., *Atsion: A Town of Four Faces*, Batsto, NJ: Batsto Citizens Committee, 1979

Gilman, John and Heide, Robert, *O'New Jersey*, New York: St. Martin's Press, 1992

Forman, Richard T.T., ed., *Pine Barrens: Ecosystem and Landscape*, New York: Academic Press, 1979

Grimm, William Carey, *The Illustrated Book of Wildflowers and Shrubs*, Harrisburg,PA: Stackpole Books, 1993

Kemp, Franklin W., *A Nest of Rebel Pirates*, Egg Harbor City, NJ: The Laureate Press, 1966

Lawrence, Susannah, *The Audubon Society Field Guide to the Natural Places of the Mid Atlantic: Coastal*, New York: Pantheon Books, 1984

Leiby, Adrian C., *The Early Dutch and Swedish Settlers of New Jersey*, Princeton: D. Van Nostrand Co., 1964

Little, Elbert L., *The Audubon Society Field Guide to North American Trees*, New York: Alfred A. Knopf, 1980

Lincoff, Gary H., *The Audubon Society Field Guide to North American Mushrooms*, New York: Alfred A. Knopf, 1992

Lloyd, John Bailey, *Eighteen Miles of History on Long Beach Island*, Harvey Cedars, NJ: Down the Shore Publishing, 1994

McGloy, James F. and Miller, Ray, *The Jersey Devil*, Wallingford, PA: The Middle Atlantic Press, 1976

McMahon, William, *South Jersey Towns*, New Brunswick: Rutgers University Press, 1973

Michalsky, B., W*hitesbog: An Historical Sketch*, Browns Mills, NJ: Conservation and Environmental Studies Center, 1978

McPhee, John, *The Pine Barrens*, New York: Farrar Straus & Giroux, 1981

Nash, Charles Edgar, *The Lure of Long Beach*, Beach Haven, NJ: Long Beach Board of Trade, 1936

Parnes, Robert, *Canoeing the Jersey Pine Barrens*, Chester, Connecticut: Globe Pequot Press, 1994

Peterson, Roger Tory, *A Field Guide to the Birds East of the Rockies*, Boston: Houghton Mifflin Company, 1980

## Bicycling

Ballantine, Richard, *Richard's New Bicycle Book*, New York: Ballantine Books, 1987

Brandt, Jobst, *The Bicycle Wheel*, Menlo Park, CA: Avocet, 1981

Forester, John, *Effective Cycling*, Palo Alto,CA: Custom Cycle Fitments, 1975

Murphy, Jim, *Two Hundred Years of Bicycles*, New York: J.B. Lippincott, 1983

Perry, David B., *Bike Cult*, New York: Four Walls Eight Windows, 1995

Ritchie, Andrew, *King of the Road: An Illustrated History of Cycling*, Berkeley: Ten Speed Press, 1975

Snowling, Steve and Evans, Ken, *Bicycle Mechanics in Workshop and Competition*, Champaign,IL: Leisure Press, 1987

Van der Plas, Rob, *The Bicycle Repair Book*, Mill Valley, CA: Bicycle Books, 1990

Weaver, Susan, *A Woman's Guide to Cycling*, Berkeley: Ten Speed Press, 1991

# Index

# K

Killcohook National Wildlife Refuge, 71
Kings Grant, 141
Kramer, Frank, 12

# L

Lakehurst Museum, 198
Lakehurst Naval Air Station, 191, 196, 198
Lake Lenape Park, 90, 91
Lebanon Glassworks, 145
Lebanon State Forest, 145, 148-149, 193
Leeds Point, 81, 99
Leesburg, 49
Lenni-Lenape, 70, 135-136
Lester G. MacNamara Wildlife Management Area, 82, 86, 91
Long Beach Island, 164, 169-176
Long Beach Island Historical Association Museum, 171
Long Beach Township, 171
Long Branch, 208-209
Loveladies, 170, 174-175
Lovelady, Thomas, 174
Lower Alloways Creek Historical Museum, 75
Lyme Disease, 17

# M

Manahawkin, 182
Manchester Wildlife Management Area, 196, 199
Manumuskin River, 10, 45, 52
Maple Lake Wildlife Management Area, 87
Maryland, 203
Maskells Mill State Wildlife Area, 75
Maurice River, 10, 45, 46, 48, 67
Mauricetown, 45, 46
Mays Landing, 89, 90, 91, 93
Meade, George, 175
Medford, 136, 139
Medford Lakes, 139

Menantico River, 10, 45
Mey, Cornelius, 24, 89, 165
Miami Beach, 31
Monmouth Beach, 209
Mott, Gershom, 73
Mount Holly, 152
Mount Misery, 145, 148
Mullica, Eric, 117
Mullica River, 112, 114, 115, 117, 118, 122, 165
Mulliner, Joe, 118
Muskee Creek, 10, 45, 52

# N

Nail House Museum, 59
Nature Conservancy, 26, 67, 195
New Brooklyn Park, 123
New Egypt, 196
New Sweden Farmstead Museum, 59
Norma, 63, 67
North Beach, 174, 176
Noyes Museum, 98, 99

# O

Ocean City, 33-35
Ocean County Historical Society, 186
Osborne Fish and Wildlife Management Area, 57
Oswego River, 128
Oyster Creek, 99
Oyster harvesting, 45-46

# P

Parvin Lake, 61, 63-64
Parvin, Lemuel, 64
Parvin State Park, 56, 60-61, 63-65, 67
Pasadena, 145, 193
Peaslee Wildlife Management Area, 52, 86
Pemberton Lake Wildlife Management Area, 146
Penn State Forest, 128, 132-133
Penn, William, 58

# About the Author

Kurt B. Detwiler has been an avid bicyclist for almost 20 years. He has accumulated thousands of miles touring the roads and trails of the Jersey Shore, Pine Barrens and Delaware Bay Region. After graduating from Gettysburg College in 1983, he worked as a bicycle mechanic, salesperson and store manager. In 1986, he studied scientific glassblowing at Salem Community College and subsequently worked as a neon tubebender. A long time New Jersey resident, the writer now lives in Pleasant Valley, Maryland. His previous books for EPM are *Bicycling Through Civil War History* and *Shifting Gears, A Bicycling Guide to West Virginia*.